AMERICA IN
WORLD WAR I

Also by the Authors

By Donald M. Goldstein and Harry J. Maihafer:
The Korean War: The Story and Photographs (2000)

By Donald M. Goldstein and Katherine V. Dillon, with
   J. Michael Wenger:
The Way It Was: Pearl Harbor: The Original Photographs (1991)
D-Day Normandy: The Story and Photographs (1993)
"Nuts!" The Battle of the Bulge: The Story and Photographs (1994)
Rain of Ruin: The Hiroshima and Nagasaki Atomic Bombs (1995)
The Vietnam War: The Story and Photographs (1997)
The Spanish-American War: The Story and Photographs (1998)

By Donald M. Goldstein and Katherine V. Dillon:
The Williwaw War (1992)
The Pearl Harbor Papers: Inside the Japanese Plans (1993)
Amelia: The Centennial Biography of an Aviation Pioneer (1997)

By Donald M. Goldstein and Katherine V. Dillon, with
   Gordon W. Prange:
At Dawn We Slept: The Untold Story of Pearl Harbor (1981)
Miracle at Midway (1982)
Target Tokyo: The Story of the Sorge Spy Ring (1984)
Pearl Harbor: The Verdict of History (1987)
December 7, 1941: The Day the Japanese Attacked Pearl Harbor (1988)
God's Samurai: Lead Pilot at Pearl Harbor (1990)

By Donald M. Goldstein and Katherine V. Dillon, with
   Masataka Chihaya:
Fading Victory: The Diary of Admiral Matome Ugaki (1991)

By Donald M. Goldstein, Phil Williams, and J. M. Shafritz:
Classic Readings of International Relations (2000)

By Donald M. Goldstein, Phil Williams, and Hank Andrews:
Security in Korea: War, Stalemate and Negation (1994)

By Harry J. Maihafer:
From the Hudson to the Yalu: West Point '49 in the Korean War (1993)
Brave Decisions: Moral Courage from the Revolutionary War to
   Desert Storm (1995)
Oblivion: The Mystery of West Point Cadet Richard Cox (1997)
The General and the Journalists: Ulysses S. Grant, Horace Greeley, and
   Charles Dana (1998)
War of Words: Abraham Lincoln and the Civil War Press (2001)

AMERICA IN
WORLD WAR I

The Story and Photographs

Donald M. Goldstein
and
Harry J. Maihafer

Potomac Books, Inc.
Washington, D.C.

Library of Congress Cataloging-in-Publication Data

Goldstein, Donald M.
   America in World War I : the story and photographs / Donald M. Goldstein
and Harry J. Maihafer.—1st ed.
        p.   cm.
   Includes bibliographical references and index.
   ISBN 1-57488-390-9 (hardcover : alk. paper)—ISBN 1-57488-615-0
(pbk. : alk. paper)
   1. World War, 1914–1918—United States—Pictorial works.   I. Title:
America in World War I.   II. Title: America in World War One.
III. Maihafer, Harry J. (Harry James), 1924–   IV. Title.

D570.G65   2003
940.3'73'0222—dc21
                                        2002156281

Printed in the United States of America on acid-free paper that meets the
American National Standards Institute Z39-48 Standard.

Potomac Books, Inc.
22841 Quicksilver Drive
Dulles, Virginia 20166

Book design and composition by Susan Mark, Coghill Composition Company
Maps by Jay Karamales

First Edition

10 9 8 7 6 5 4 3 2 1

Contents

Maps

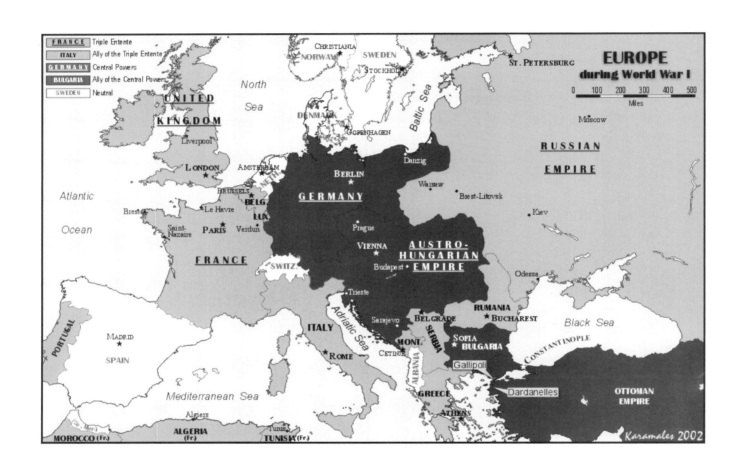

Preface

This is the eighth in Brassey's series of photographic books titled "America Goes to War." Six of the previous volumes were written by Donald M. Goldstein, Katherine V. Dillon, and J. Michael Wenger. These previous volumes were: *The Way It Was: Pearl Harbor, D-Day Normandy, "Nuts!": The Battle of the Bulge, Rain of Ruin: A Photographic History of Hiroshima and Nagasaki, The Vietnam War,* and *The Spanish American War. The Korean War* and this volume were written by Donald M. Goldstein and Harry J. Maihafer, a graduate of the U.S. Military Academy at West Point, a retired Army officer, and a combat veteran who passed away before this work was completed.

We divided the current volume into twelve chapters. Chapter 1, "Europe Ablaze," describes the war in Europe before the United States's entry. Chapter 2, "America Enters the Ring," describes the events leading to the United States's decision to enter the war. Chapter 3, "The War at Sea," relates the early days of the war at sea and the American decision to enter the war because of German U-boat actions. Chapter 4, "Getting the Boys 'Over There,'" depicts the largest mobilization up to that time in U.S. history. Chapter 5, "Training in France," shows how U.S. ground forces trained and were integrated into the war effort. Chapter 6, "Tools of War," describes some of the weapons used by both sides that made this one of the bloodiest wars in history and which led to many modern-day weapons. Chapter 7, "Yanks in the Trenches," describes U.S. involvement during her early days in the war. Chapter 8, "The Home Front," describes Americans at home during the war. Chapter 9, "The Crucial Months: March–July 1918," relates the harsh fighting that took place during the last days of the war and the American contributions to the war effort. Chapter 10, "The Air War," depicts this new and modern phase of warfare that was the birth of the airplane in combat. Emphasis is placed on the roles of Eddie Rickenbacker and the Red Baron (Baron von Richtofen). Chapter 11, "Meuse-Argonne, the Final Push: August–November 1918," relates the final months of the war. Chapter 12, "The Aftermath," discusses the Versailles Treaty and its consequences.

Although we attempt to present the story of "the Great War" in the context of its political and diplomatic background, this is primarily the story of American participation. Time and space preclude us from talking about America's allies, though we do not wish to diminish their contribution to the war, which was much greater than that of the United States. For other books on the entire war, we refer you to our bibliography.

All photographs in this book are in the public domain. They are located at the National Archives, College Park, Maryland; the Army War College, Carlisle Barracks, Pennsylvania; or they are the personal property of the authors. Queries about the latter should be directed to Donald M. Goldstein.

We are gratefully indebted to James Enos who helped us with the photographic work and to Matthew Keller and Judith Williams for their help in researching the book. Special thanks to Lisa Gillette and Emily Walker, Donald Goldstein's associates who did yeomen work in helping to research and tie the book together; to Katherine V. Dillon, Goldstein's longtime partner and coauthor who read the manuscript and offered useful comments; to Jack Grater for all his support; to Kendall Stanley for her typing and editing; and to Don McKeon and Don Jacobs at Brassey's who, as usual, made it all happen. Finally, kudos to my wife, Mariann, and to Jeanne Maihafer, who always encouraged us through thick and thin to finish.

Mr. Maihafer and I originally planned to dedicate this book to the Americans who fought and died in the Great War, may their sacrifices never be forgotten. However, I would like to make a special dedication to my colleague Harry Maihafer, soldier, businessman, scholar, author, and above all a true friend who represents what this whole series, "America Goes to War," is all about.

Donald M. Goldstein, Ph.D.
Professor of Public and International Affairs
University of Pittsburgh
Pittsburgh, Pennsylvania

Introduction

The collision toward which Europe had been heading for more than a decade came in the summer of 1914. The causes behind the outbreak of the war in August 1914 were complex and, even today, highly controversial. There were, however, three elements of immediate significance in transferring what might have been only another political assassination into the holocaust of 1914–1918: the desire of several European states to prove their great power status, the complexities of the rigid alliance system that developed after the turn of the century, and the intricacies of modern military mobilization.

European states had sought to maintain a balance of power on the continent since the defeat of Napoléon in 1815. The victors, led by Austria and Great Britain, devised a system in which the nations would maneuver and align themselves so that no single nation would become excessively powerful. By 1907, however, the system was failing, and the balance of power was replaced by a rigid two-camp system that pitted the Triple Alliance (Germany, Austria-Hungary, and Italy) against the Triple Entente (France, Russia, and Great Britain).

Adding to the volatile atmosphere that pervaded Europe were the national objectives that drove each of the powers. The two oldest empires, Austria-Hungary and Russia, sought to assert their Great Power status; the former by attempting to consolidate its power in the Balkans by subduing its subject peoples, the latter by asserting its self-assigned role as the protector of the Slavic people in southeastern Europe.

Germany, economically and militarily, the dominant power on the continent, was obsessed by a national inferiority complex. The Germans felt that they were not granted the great power status they deserved, and the government often assumed a belligerent tone with other nations. Encircled by the Franco-Russian alliance, Germany felt compelled to support Austria lest she be left stranded diplomatically and militarily. France, still smarting from the loss of her territory to Germany in 1870–71, rent by internal difficulties, and recognizing the growing power of Germany, was convinced she had to support her ally Russia in order to insulate herself against an aggressive neighbor. Finally, Britain while seeking to maintain its traditional separation from the continent, did not want to see Germany become the dominant land power in Europe at the same time the Germans were increasing their maritime fleet and navy.

The spark that touched off the powder keg of complex motives and intricate alliances was the assassination of the heir to the throne of the Austro-Hungarian Empire, the Archduke Franz Ferdinand and his wife, during a visit to Sarajevo, the provincial capital of Bosnia, on June 28, 1914. The assassin was a member of a Slavic nationalist organization that sought to separate the province of Bosnia from the Austro-Hungarian Empire and make it part of independent Serbia. Conscious that it was losing its status as a major power and fearful that the empire would fragment if the insistent pressure from the subject-nationalities was not quelled, Austria resolved to make an issue of these murders.

Three weeks after Franz Ferdinand's death, the Austrian government sent Serbia an ultimatum demanding that Austrian police and armed forces be allowed to enter Serbia to help clean out the Slavic nationalist group that instigated the assassinations. In this stand, Germany backed Austria-Hungary; Russia stood by Serbia.

For four weeks there was a flurry of diplomatic activity designed to reassure allies and to forestall opponents. However, rebuffed by Serbia, Austria-Hungary declared war on July 28. Russia, refusing to heed Germany's warning that mobilization would mean war, started to mobilize the next day after rejecting a German ultimatum to stand down. Russia's mobilization convinced Germany that it had to go to war, which meant going to war with France as well. Germany declared war on Russia on August 1, 1914, forcing a full French mobilization. Two days later Germany declared war on France. That same day German armies invaded neutral Belgium, thereby drawing Britain into the war on the side of France and Russia against Germany and Austria-Hungary. Turkey would ally with Germany and Austria by the end of the year.

The course of mobilization was not the only consideration that affected the decisions of the various powers: war plans themselves determined political decisions. The most significant was the German's famous Schlieffen Plan. Organized to the minutest detail, the plan depended upon speed and execution and gave the German army no room for error. In the early weeks of the war, the plan was successful. But as German troops were attempting to carry out the planned encirclement of Paris, Russian troops were massing on Germany's eastern border more quickly than German planners had expected. This caused the German General Staff to break with the Schlieffen Plan, which had called for concentrating on the defeat of France, and divert troops to face the Russians. Although the Germans defeated the Russians in the east, they were never able to capture Paris. After several months of terrible fighting, the Western Front bogged down and produced a war of attrition characterized by trench warfare. After the first three years of the war (1914–1917), neither side was victorious. The war on the Western Front became a bloody stalemate until the tide turned with the arrival of fresh U.S. troops.

In the years leading up to the war, the United States had been busy filling out its borders and expanding its influence abroad. The Spanish American War of 1898–99 made the United States a world power, with new territories in Asia and the Caribbean. Oklahoma became a state in 1907, and Arizona and New Mexico followed suit in 1913 and 1914, respectively. George Washington in his farewell address had warned the country to stay out of European entanglements, and the country was still trying to heed his advice. Woodrow Wilson, re-elected president in 1916 on a ticket to keep the United States out of war, was determined to succeed. However, pressure from a strong pro-British group and the sinking of U.S. ships by German submarines added to the public outrage created after the British intercepted the infamous Zimmerman Telegram (which promised Mexico the possible return of Arizona, New Mexico, and Texas if they came into the fray on the side of Germany). The United States was shocked into reconsidering its isolationist position. U.S. Army General John Pershing was already having trouble on the Mexican border with Pancho Villa, a Mexican renegade. President Wilson asked Congress for a declaration of war against Germany. The United States entered the war to end all wars on April 6, 1917, and became the deciding force that broke the war of attrition.

This is the story of the U.S. contribution to World War I as depicted by the hundreds of photographs available.

ONE

Europe Ablaze

Europe Ablaze

In August 1914, U.S. news-papers told their startled read-ers that war had broken out in Europe. Guns were booming and the situation was grave [1-1]. For the average American, how-ever, like the St. Louis citizens shown in photo 1-2, it was still "business as usual." Events 3,000 miles away, on the far side of a broad ocean, had little impact on everyday life, and there seemed no reason for America to become involved. American President Woodrow Wilson, reflecting the public mood, told Congress that the United States should remain neutral, saying, "we must be impartial in thought as well as action" [1-3]. Like people in the rest of the country, Washingtoni-ans agreed. In the nation's capi-tal, in fact, men were more concerned with "Big Train" Walter Johnson, the fabled Washington Senators pitcher who had won thirty-six games the previous year but who might be tailing off. In the 1914 season, he would win "only" twenty-eight [1-4].

1-1 German troops marching through Belgium.

1-2 Business as usual in St. Louis, 1914.

1-3 President Woodrow Wilson.

1-4 Walter Johnson.

1-5 Archduke Franz Ferdinand and his wife, Sophie, in Sarajevo shortly before their assassination.

The European crisis had begun five weeks earlier, when a Serbian terrorist, Gavrilo Princip, assassinated Austrian Archduke Franz Ferdinand and his wife at Sarajevo in the Austrian province of Bosnia [1-5], a place very few Americans had heard of and even fewer could have located on a map. Austria-Hungary blamed the small kingdom of Serbia for the assassination, although the Austrians did not have proof at the time. But the chief of the Serbian army's general staff was indeed involved in the plot, and Austria felt it was forced to retaliate against Serbia. Doing so, however, might cause the Russian Czar Nicholas to come to the aid of his "Slav brothers" [1-6]. The possibility of confrontation with Russia caused the Austro-Hungarian Emperor, Franz Josef [1-7], to line up support of his own by calling on his ally, Germany's Kaiser Wilhelm II [1-8]. This brought into play what was to prove a tragic network of interlocking mutual assistance treaties. France and Russia were pledged to help each

1-6 Czar Nicholas II of Russia and his son, Alexi.

1-7 Emperor Franz Josef of Austria.

1-8 Kaiser Wilhelm II of Germany.

1-9 Czar Nicholas II (left) and King George V of England in German uniform.

1-10 Admiral Alfred von Tirpitz, commander-in-chief of the German Navy.

other if either was attacked by Germany. England would help France if the vital interests of both were threatened. Germany, Austria-Hungary, and Italy (the Triple Alliance) would go to war together if any one of them was attacked by two other states. Italy, however, would remain on the sidelines for several months.

Each country wanted to be seen as pursuing peace. Mobilizing, however, by calling reservists to active duty and moving troops to neighboring borders, would be seen as a hostile act. Nevertheless, no one wanted to be the last to prepare. Accordingly, in the tumultuous weeks that followed, European countries, one after another, began to mobilize, plunging down a precipitous slope that, in hindsight, appears unnecessary, avoidable, and full of miscalculations.

As war clouds gathered, cooler heads tried to calm the situation. In England, King

George V [1-9] supposedly told his cousin, Kaiser Wilhelm's brother, Prince Henry, "We shall try all we can to keep out of this and shall remain neutral." Because of language difficulties, this may have been misunderstood. Nevertheless, in the early stages of the crisis, it convinced the Kaiser that

England would not intervene. When German Admiral Tirpitz [1-10] said he doubted that England would remain neutral, the Kaiser answered, "The word of a king is good enough for me."

Elsewhere in England, Lord of the Admiralty Winston Churchill was proposing to the British cabinet that European sovereigns "be brought together for the sake of peace" [1-11]. Unfortunately nothing tangible came of this, nor was any other voice of prudence able to prevail. After declaring war on Serbia on July 28, Austria decided to mobilize against Russia on July 30. On August 1, Russia began to mobilize for war against Austria and Germany. Austria's mobilization compelled the Kaiser and Chancellor Bethmann-Hollweg to allow the German military to implement the Schlieffen Plan, which went into effect after the Russian order to mobilize.

1-11 Winston Churchill, First Sea Lord, inspecting British Royal Navy cadets.

1-12 King Albert I.

Europe was like a runaway train, loaded with explosives and careening toward disaster.

By August 4, 1914, the day Britain declared war on Germany, Europe was in a state of general war. Belgium, France, Russia, and Britain (the "Allies") were at war against Germany and Austria-Hungary (the "Central Powers"). Austria was at war with Serbia, and Belgium was being overrun by the German offensive on the Western Front.

How did America react to all this? Initially at least, the overwhelming mood was a desire not to be "sucked in." Early in the war a *Literary Digest* poll of 367 writers and editors showed 105 favored the Allies and 20 favored the Central Powers, but a clear majority, 242, favored neutrality.

The Germans, having rejected Belgium's neutrality agreement as a "scrap of paper" and expecting only token resistance, were surprised by Belgian determination. Belgian King Albert I [1-12] had quickly mobilized his comparatively small army, although he urged civilians to stay out of the fighting and give the Germans no excuse for reprisals. Nevertheless, civilian nonresistance did little or nothing to placate the invaders. In many instances, villages were burned, and innocent civilians were shot. Even the university town of Louvain, the famed "Oxford of Belgium," was subjected to burning and looting. The Louvain library, with its priceless 230,000 books, was burnt out; 1,100 other buildings were destroyed; 209 civilians killed; and the population of 42,000 forcibly evacuated. As word of these events reached the outside world, there were howls of outrage. In America and elsewhere, committees were formed to provide relief to Belgian refugees.

In the following days, as Germans swept through Belgium and on into France, 90,000 British troops, commanded by General Sir John French [1-13], landed on the continent and joined forces with the French. Nevertheless, the Allies were forced back, almost to the gates of Paris. Then, at the Marne River, the German offensive shuddered to a halt as the Allies gained the initiative. At one point, the French General Josef Joffre, in his report to French commander Ferdinand Foch

1-13 General Sir John French, commander of the British Expeditionary Force at the start of the war.

quoted as saying, "My right is driven in, my center is giving way, the situation is excellent, I attack" [1-14]. The first battle of

1-14 French General Josef Joffre and French Commander Ferdinand Foch.

1-15 The famous Field Marshal Alfred von Schlieffen, architect of Germany's plan for fighting a two-front war.

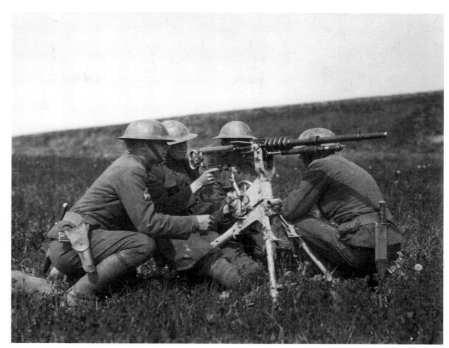

1-16 A British machine gun crew.

the Marne began September 6 and was over by September 10, with the Germans in retreat, not to regroup until they had fallen back some sixty miles. This allowed the English Channel ports to remain in Allied hands, guaranteeing communications between England and France. For the moment, Paris was saved, and the Allies were given time to muster their resources.

The elaborate German war plan, developed years earlier by Field Marshal Alfred von Schlieffen [1-15], had envisioned a fast moving offensive and a quick victory. Thanks to French, British, and Belgian resistance, and faster-than-expected mobilization by Russia, this had not happened. Germany's scheme of dealing France a knockout blow, then turning all its strength against Russia, had

become but a dream of the past. Both sides now foresaw a lengthy struggle.

Generals began to realize that this had become a different kind of war, one dominated by the defense. The killing power of the new magazine rifles and machine

guns had changed the face of battle [1-16]. Before the war, for example, it was thought that cavalry [1-17] would continue to play a vital role in future conflicts. Germany, Russia, and France had all expanded their mounted arm. Cavalrymen

1-17 French cavalry units moving to the front. Note: The cavalry men are not mounted and are wearing plumed helmets and carrying weapons.

1-18 German wagon trains moving to the front.

carrying lances, often wearing plumed helmets, were no match for automatic weapons, however, and the war would see the abandonment of horse cavalry units as a combat arm. For the most part, the noble horse would be relegated to far less glamorous roles such as transporting individual officers or towing supply wagons [1-18].

Armies began digging in, and it became a war fought from the trenches [1-19]. Gains now were measured not in miles, but in yards. Attacks and counterattacks, in the face of artillery and small arms fire, became more and more costly. On the Western Front, in what partipants later referred to as the first battle of Ypres, casualties reached ghastly proportions. Weeks earlier, as men had marched off to war, they had thought the coming struggle would be a short, romantic adventure. Face to face with the stark, ugly reality of the battlefield, they no longer heard tunes of glory, and for most of them, the war lost its appeal. Nevertheless, in early November, when young German Lance Corporal Adolf Hitler was awarded an Iron Cross Second Class, he wrote his former landlord, "It was the happiest day of my life" [1-20].

By the end of 1914 the opposing armies, facing each other across what was called "No Man's Land," had established a continuous line of trenches, 475 miles long, reaching from the North Sea to the frontier of neutral Switzerland. In the first five months of the war, French casualties alone were some 300,000 dead and 600,000 wounded. France would see no more battles in the conventional sense. Men were being killed or maimed every day, but the battlefield itself was mostly bare since machine guns and artillery made any movement above ground almost foolhardy. No trees grew in "No Man's Land," and no building

1-19 A 1st Lancashire Fusiliers' communication trench, June 1916.

1-20 Lance Corporal Adolf Hitler (right) and German Army friends.

1-21 General Paul von Hindenburg.

sians, with massive superiority in numbers, were expected to wear down the Germans. Then in the fall of 1914, German forces led by Generals Paul von Hindenburg [1-21] and Erich Ludendorff [1-22] split the Czar's advancing forces in East Prussia and won a decisive victory at Tannenberg. They drove the Russians out of East Prussia and were soon

remained unscathed. In one sense it was siege warfare, except neither side was truly besieged.

The prospect of a significant offensive appeared remote as winter set in at the end of 1914. Not only were both sides physically exhausted by human loss, there were also severe shortages of ammunition; the previous four months had nearly used up their peacetime stocks, and production facilities were not yet in full gear.

European armies had started the war thinking about attacking the enemy's flanks. Now, with a continuous line established and anchored, those flanks had ceased to exist. And frontal attacks offered little promise, at least for the foreseeable future. Commanders now realized that major artillery support was required for such attacks, and all armies were short of guns and ammunition. A kind of lull settled over the battlefield as men crouched down in the trenches and licked their wounds. At home and in the trenches, people admitted to themselves that it would be a long war. All thoughts of a quick victory had vanished.

On the Eastern Front the Rus-

1-22 General Erich von Ludendorff.

1-23 Enver Pasha, Turkish minister of war.

advancing rapidly into the Russian provinces of Poland, which had been annexed by Russia in the eighteenth century. Germany's partner, Austria, was less fortunate, and the Russians overran the Austrian province of Galicia, taking thousands of prisoners. Meanwhile the war was spreading. Eventually World War I, "The Great War," would be fought not only in Europe but also in Africa, Asia, the Middle East, and on the high seas. In Europe, there would be the Western Front, where most Americans would see action, and also an Italian, Macedonian, and Eastern Front. Inevitably other countries were drawn into the conflict, including Turkey, which by the end of 1914 was aligned with Germany and Austria-Hungary [1-23]. For their part in the fight against the Central Powers, the Allies hoped to enlist the help not only of Greece and Rumania, but

also Italy. The Germans and Austrians were also looking for help, particularly against Russia, and Bulgaria joined the Central Powers in 1915. German efforts to weaken Russia included helping the dissident Bolsheviks, who eventually took Russia out of the war in late 1917.

In 1915 the bloodbath continued on the Western Front, but without appreciable gains by either side. That year also saw the introduction of ghastly new instruments of war such as flamethrowers. In January 1915 poison gas (chlorine) made its first appearance when the Germans used it against the Russians. Later in 1915, as Germans defeated the British in the Second Battle of Ypres, they used even deadlier gases, including phosgene and mustard. At first, gasses could be used only when there was a favorable wind blowing toward enemy lines because they were released from cannisters. Later, chemical artillery shells were

developed. By the end of the war, one shell in four would be chemical, and the gas mask would be part of each soldier's standard equipment [1-24, 1-25].

Trench systems became heavily fortified and more elaborate, with mines laid in profusion. Barbed wire, invented by American cattle ranchers in the 1870s, began to appear strung in belts between the opposing trenches. Underground shelters, called "dugouts," were also prepared and reinforced.

To the east, a British naval expedition was launched against Turkey in an attempt to capture Istanbul and open the Bosporus Straits to the Black Sea, thus allowing communication with Russia. This was the "Gallipoli" expedition, which ended in dismal failure after many heartbreaking months. It had been conceived in Britain, notably by Winston Churchill, who took much of the blame, a blame that lingered for years.

1-24 British soldiers blinded by German gas making their way to dressing stations.

1-25 British soldiers wearing typical gas masks.

In May 1915, heretofore neutral Italy declared war on Austria-Hungary. For Italy the timing was atrocious. Germany would soon drive the Russians out of Galicia and much of Poland. These actions cost Russia one million men in prisoners and two million casualties. Romania was also conquered, and with the Balkan flank protected, the Central Powers turned to Italy, dealing it a paralyzing blow at Caporetto in the fall of 1917.

Under international law, the United States was permitted to ship supplies not listed as "contraband of war" to neutral countries, such as Holland or Denmark, where they might be forwarded to Germany. A British North Sea blockade, however, declaring nearly everything "contraband of war," effectively cut Germany off from outside assistance. Meanwhile, with neutral countries, notably the U.S., shipping supplies to

Britain, Germany retaliated by announcing the existence of a war zone around the British Isles. All were warned of the dangers that neutral vessels faced in those waters, and to carry out this threat, Germany, with its fleet bottled up, said it would rely on its *Unterseeboots*, the submarines commonly known as U-boats [1-26, 1-27].

American public opinion began to swing more and more in favor of the Allies, especially after the Cunard luxury liner *Lusitania* was sunk on May 7, 1915. Of the 1,257 passengers, 159 were Americans, of whom 124 perished [1-28]. Eleven days earlier, the German government had informed the American Secretary of State William Jennings Bryan [1-29] that the *Lusitania*, when it sailed from New York, would be carrying six million rounds of rifle ammunition manufactured by Remington for British Enfield rifles. A message warning

1-26 German U-boat, L.M. Unterseeboot I, in action.

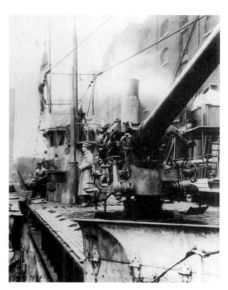

1-27 The deck of a German U-boat up close.

1-28 The Cunard Liner *Lusitania*.

1-29 President Wilson's first secretary of state, Williams Jennings Bryan.

passengers, cleared by Bryan and bordered in black, had appeared in New York papers on May 1, along with Cunard's announcement of the scheduled ship sailing. Nevertheless, Cunard spokesmen said there were no more than the usual number of last-minute cancellations.

Secretary Bryan saw the incident realistically, saying, "A ship carrying contraband should not rely upon passengers to protect her from attack—it would be like putting women and children in front of an army." Few shared his view, and President Wilson, calling the sinking "unlawful and inhuman," fired off sharp notes.

Ignoring the fact that the ship was carrying illegal contraband, the *New York Herald* was typical, saying the sinking was "premeditated murder." President Wilson called it "unlawful and inhuman," firing off sharp notes to the Germans and demanding reparations. Bryan resigned in protest over the note, and Robert Lansing [1-30] was named the new secretary of state. American passions were inflamed. Nevertheless, three days after the sinking, Wilson told a Philadelphia audience that "There is such a thing as a man being too proud to fight" [1-31 to 1-34].

In April 1916, President Wilson formally protested the

1-30 Robert Lansing, who succeeded Bryan as secretary of state.

1-31 *Lusitania* survivors.

1-32 German U-139, which sank the *Lusitania*.

1-33 German U-77.

1-34 German U-139.

resistance." For a time, Germany honored this pledge, allowing merchant ships not carrying contraband to pass unmolested [1-36]. Also, when ships were sunk, U-boat captains made an effort to rescue survivors [1-37]. For the moment, America was conciliated.

American attitudes continued to be affected, however, by tales of German atrocities such as the execution of Edith Cavell, a British Red Cross nurse in Brussels, who helped some 200 Allied soldiers to escape through the Netherlands. Some of the stories were evidently true, but others, such as German soldiers bayoneting babies or amputating the hands of Belgian boys or the breasts of Belgian women, were patently false; many of them had been planted by clever Allied propagandists. The end result

continued German submarine sinkings and what he viewed as a clear violation of international law. In response, Germany said it would abandon "unrestricted submarine warfare" but reserved the right to initiate it again at its own discretion. German Chancellor Bethmann-Hollweg [1-35] pledged that merchant ships would "not be sunk without warning and without saving human lives unless such ships attempt to escape or offer

1-35 German Chancellor Theobald von Bethmann-Hollweg.

1-36, 1-37 German U-boats helping to rescue enemy (Allied) survivors.

was that many Americans began to believe the German "Hun" was a barbarian [1-38].

In France, massive offensives were launched to end the stalemate. Over a five-month period, German forces were hurled against French defenses centered on Verdun. The French cried, "they shall not pass," a slogan that gained an almost mystic appeal, and the French were able to hold. When the German high command finally gave the order to call off the offensive, 300,000 German lives had been sacrificed in vain. French casualties were also heavy, but the attack had been blunted, and Germany had gained only some 130 square miles. The Allies then struck with a counteroffensive aimed at German forces along the Somme River. From July 1916 until the following November, the attack continued relentlessly, but the Germans held, and the Somme offensive was also a failure. The campaigns of 1916 had cost more than a million lives, with no important gains for either side. Exhausted, and with sagging morale, the opposing armies settled into a miserable war of mud and dirt, fought from fortified, increasingly miserable trenches [1-39]. On January 9, 1917, over the objections of his chancellor, the Kaiser was persuaded by Hindenburg and Ludendorff to renounce the pledge to abandon unrestricted submarine warfare [1-40]. Although Germany realized this might bring the U.S. into the conflict, their leaders believed the war would be over before America could have any effect on its outcome. On January 22, the humanitarian Woodrow Wilson told the Senate that he would call for "a peace without victory." It was pure idealism, although many shared Wilson's pacifist philosophy. One of the most popular songs on Tin Pan Alley would be "I Didn't Raise My Boy to Be a Soldier."

Finally bowing to reality, Wilson broke diplomatic relations with Germany on February 3. Before the month was out, he

1-38 French poster remembering the death of Nurse Edith Cavell in Brussels, October 1915.

1-39 Two German officers making their way through a muddy communications trench.

asked Congress for "extraordinary powers" to maintain an armed neutrality and to permit the arming of merchant ships. On March 1, Wilson released to the press a diplomatic bombshell, the "Zimmermann Telegram." The message had been intercepted by the British, decoded, and then passed on to the White House. In it, Alfred Zimmermann [1-41], the German undersecretary of foreign affairs, had instructed his ambassador in Mexico to propose a German–Mexican alliance in case the U.S. declared war on Germany. It contained the proviso that "Mexico is to reconquer the lost territory in New Mexico, Texas, and Arizona," and further asked Mexico to urge Japan to join the Central Powers—Germany, Austria-Hungary, Bulgaria, and Turkey. For U.S. public opinion, it was the last straw.

Woodrow Wilson had just started his second term, reelected on the slogan that "he kept us out of war." It was reluctantly, then, and with a heavy heart, that on the evening of April 3, 1917, he called on Congress for a declaration of war, saying the United States must fight "for the ultimate peace of the world and the liberation of its people. . . . The world must be made safe

1-40 Left to right: Hindenburg, Wilhelm, and Ludendorff.

1-41 Alfred Zimmerman, German undersecretary of foreign affairs.

for democracy." His speech was greeted with resounding applause.

After returning to the White House later that night, Wilson and his wife had dinner with friends. Then the president wandered off. His secretary, Joseph Tumulty, found him later, sitting at the table in the Cabinet Room. Looking up, Wilson said, "Think what it was they were applauding. My message today was a message of death for our young men. How strange it seems to applaud that." Then the peace-loving Wilson put his head down on the table and sobbed.

TWO

America Enters the Ring

America Enters the Ring

On April 5, 1917, two days after Woodrow Wilson's appearance before Congress, the Senate voted for war by 82 to 6. The following day, the House followed suit by a 373 to 50 vote. That afternoon the president signed the declaration putting America at war with Germany. (War was not declared on Austria-Hungary until eight months later.)

The news was flashed to the country and greeted with enthusiasm. Thousands of patriotic young men headed for recruiting offices. In Great Neck, Long Island, the songwriter and playwright George M. Cohan was inspired to compose the song "Over There." He took it to the popular vaudeville star Nora Bayes, who sang it that night to a cheering audience. Its vigorous words burst with enthusiasm and confidence:

Over there, over there
Send the word, send the word,
    over there
That the Yanks are coming, the
    Yanks are coming

The drum tum-tumming
    everywhere
So prepare, say a pray'r
Send the word, send the word,
    to beware
We'll be over, we're coming
    over
And we won't be back 'til it's
    over, over there.

It would become the most popular song of the war [2-1].

At this stage, few realized the vast difference between a willingness to fight and an ability to do so. Actually the country was ill prepared militarily, either in trained manpower or equipment. Americans traditionally had opposed a large standing army, viewing such a thing almost with suspicion. The army had only 5,000 officers and 120,000 enlisted men, plus some 80,000 ill-trained and poorly equipped national guardsmen. Few had ever heard a shot fired in anger. Among the world's armies, the U.S. ranked sixteenth in size, just behind Portugal. The United States had no tanks, its fifty or so planes were nearly obsolete, and its

heavy guns had ammunition enough for only a nine-hour bombardment. Moreover, there was a critical shortage of machine guns and mobile artillery, the most effective killing tools of the Western Front.

In April 1917, the army's chief of staff was General Hugh L. Scott, an able, intelligent man who had served many years on the frontier during the Indian

2-1 Poster promoting "Over There," the most popular song of the war in America.

2-2 General Hugh L. Scott.

wars [2-2]. He was sixty-three years old, as was his deputy, General Tasker H. Bliss, an equally able man. Both men, however, were nearing retirement age and were admittedly unfamiliar with the technology and tactics of the Western Front.

To assist him when the war started, Scott had a general staff numbering only fifty-one officers, and because of an unrealistic law, only nineteen of these could be stationed in Washington, D.C. By contrast, in August 1914, when war began in Europe, the British had 234 officers on their general staff, the French 644, and the Germans 650.

Not everyone was surprised by the country's lack of preparedness. The War College, in a study published in 1915, had said America needed a standing army of at least 500,000 men plus a fully equipped reserve of equal strength. It further said that it would take eighteen to twenty-four months just to arm and equip such a force. Above all, the study said, trained manpower would be required. Despite this lack of capability, former president Theodore Roosevelt had been saying for months that the United States should have already joined the fight. In September 1915 he accused his fellow Americans of

2-3 A young Theodore Roosevelt.

shirking their moral responsibilities. "The United States has played a most ignoble part for the last thirteen months," Roosevelt said. "Our Government has declined to keep its plighted faith, has declined to take action for justice and right, as it was pledged to take action under the Hague conventions. At the same time, it has refused to protect its own citizens; and it has refused even to prepare for its own defense." He might be older, but he'd lost none of the aggressiveness he's shown as a "Roughrider" during the Spanish-American War [2-3].

In March 1917, with war clouds on the horizon, Congress passed a Conscription Act authorizing a military draft. On May 19, Wilson signed it into law, requiring all men between the ages of twenty-one and twenty-nine to register. The age range was later extended to between eighteen and thirty-five.

2-4 President Wilson drawing numbers from a glass bowl in the first round of conscription.

2-5 Secretary of War Newton Baker drawing the first number for the second round of conscription.

50,000 carpenters and 150,000 other workers hastily slapping together hundreds of wooden barracks. Then there was the question of clothing, where huge quantities of uniforms, underwear, socks, etc., had to be ordered and produced. Many a man had to wait before being properly equipped. In the words of Hugh Johnson, a senior supply officer, "The supply situation was as nearly a perfect mess as can be imagined."

In addition to clothing, the greatest problem was the lack of equipment and qualified trainers. Nearly all the officers and noncommissioned officers of the regular army were forced to serve as instructors, and few of them would end up overseas. One who was frustrated by this was young Captain Dwight Eisenhower [2-7], who had volunteered for combat but whose orders sent him to Camp Colt, on the edge of the historic Gettysburg battlefield.

Choices for induction were made by lottery, with a blindfolded President Wilson and Secretary of War Newton Baker among those pulling numbers from a glass bowl [2-4, 2-5]. Married men were exempted, but anyone rushing into marriage to avoid conscription was thwarted—marriages after April 6, 1917, did not count.

For the most part, the draft was well received; in the patriotic aura of 1917, no one wanted to be considered a "slacker," a term coined in England for British citizens in America who failed to return to Britain in order to serve. There was however a small percentage of conscientious objectors, some of whom were drafted and placed in noncombat jobs. Canada helped the U.S. draft by closing its borders to American men of military age.

Recruits, both volunteers and draftees, were soon arriving at reception centers and being sent to training camps [2-6]. It was not an easy task. At the beginning of the war, for example, the army had no place to house the new arrivals. Therefore a Quartermaster Cantonment division was created, and a massive building program was undertaken, with as many as

2-6 Civilian draftees file into a barracks and emerge looking somewhat like soldiers.

2-7 Young Captain Dwight Eisenhower.

2-8 General Leonard Wood.

2-9 General John Pershing.

Eisenhower's job was to train tankers, although initially he had no tanks. Being forced to improvise, he taught men to drive trucks, figuring they could later learn more easily to drive tanks. To teach tank gunnery, he had machine guns bolted to flatbed trucks and had men fire at targets as the trucks drove over bumpy ground.

The junior officer problem would have been worse had it not been for the prewar Military Training Camps Association (MTCA), the so-called Plattsburgh training camps. These camps, organized by the far-sighted General Leonard Wood [2-8], gave a month-long military indoctrination to aspiring officers. After war was declared, these camps provided a basis for the officer training schools that produced second lieutenants, the so-called "ninety-day wonders."

Wood naturally hoped he would be the man selected to lead an American Expeditionary Force when the time came. There were only six major generals on active duty, and four of these were in their sixties, nearing retirement, and presumably out of contention. Wilson, however, would select General John J. Pershing for the task, even though the forty-seven-year-old Pershing, West Point Class of 1886, was junior to Wood and slightly older [2-9]. Although each man was an excellent officer, Wilson felt unsure about Wood. This was a man who would take orders, as would any career soldier, but who might also be inclined to exceed those orders. Also—and this was something Wilson could *not* overlook—Wood had on occasion not only criticized administration policies, but had done so openly. Wilson told Sec-

retary of War Baker he had "no confidence either in General Wood's discretion or in his loyalty to his superiors." Baker in turn considered Wood "the most insubordinate general in the entire army."

John "Black Jack" Pershing, had been born in Laclede, Missouri, and had grown up on a farm. After graduating from West Point, where he was first captain and president of his class, Pershing had demonstrated his leadership ability in a wide range of situations and assignments—as a lieutenant in an African-American cavalry unit (where he acquired the nickname "Black Jack"), as teacher of military science at the University of Nebraska, as commandant of cadets at West Point, and as a military attaché in Tokyo. Theodore Roosevelt had recognized his ability early on and had promoted him directly from captain to brigadier general. He had thereby leapfrogged many senior officers he would later command in France. In more recent years, as a general he had served with distinction in the Philippines and in Mexico. He was a strict disciplinarian, one who would always be respected but seldom loved. According to Robert Bullard, who would become one of Pershing's senior commanders in France, his exercise of authority was "peculiarly impersonal, dispassionate, hard and firm." However, Bullard later wrote, "This quality did not in him, as in many, give offence; the man was too impersonal, too given over to pure business and duty. His manner carried to the mind of those under him the suggestion, nay, the conviction, of unquestioned right to obedience."

Moreover, unlike Wood, Pershing's loyalty and discretion were never in doubt. Even when he was leading the Mexican Punitive Expedition against the bandit Pancho Villa [2-10], and though he was often frustrated by Wilson's policies, no word of complaint was ever voiced. For example, when told to pull out of Mexico, an order with which he violently disagreed, Pershing gave the order to withdraw without any complaint or explanation, not even to his staff. Wilson appreciated that.

In 1917, unlike in World War II, there were no basic training camps per se. Instead, a man was sent directly to a prospective combat division for training, an outfit which would stay intact, and in which the man would presumably serve until the end of the war. Of course it didn't always work out that way. In practice, units were often cannibalized as key noncoms or officers were pulled to serve as trainers and men with special skills were assigned to other duties. In addition, the goal was for each man to have at least six months stateside before going overseas. This too wasn't always feasible; many recruits were rushed overseas without even learning the basic "school of the soldier," such things as close order drill, personal hygiene, care of arms and equipment, military courtesy, and guard mount. Some would land in France without ever having fired a rifle.

America was still a rural society, and farm boys made up the largest percentage of the recruits. They made good soldiers, but were less educated, took

2-10 The Mexican bandit Pancho Villa.

2-11, 2-12, 2-13 Physical training for new recruits.

longer to train, and were often illiterate. Surprisingly, many did not know how to play any games. Their physical training often took the form of leapfrog, three-legged races, or something similar [2-11 to 2-13]. For other young soldiers, however, a baseball game was still the favorite activity [2-14].

Of troops destined for France, the best trained may have been the U.S. Marines [2-15, 2-16]. They, like their army comrades, knew that Pershing did not approve of the immobile Western Front, which he called a "meat grinder." Pershing considered trench warfare defeatist, and called on trainers to emphasize the rifle and the bayonet as "the supreme weapons of the infantry soldier." This meant an emphasis on discipline, rifle marksmanship, bayonet training, and small-unit, mobile tactics [2-17, 2-18]. In essence, Pershing wanted men who could "shoot and salute."

Pershing was directed to assemble a division-size unit for movement overseas. He would be its commander. Under army doctrine, an infantry division, with about 28,000 men, would contain two brigades, each of which would contain two regiments. (Hence the name "square division.") Each regiment would have two or more battalions, as well as the necessary service units (ordnance, quartermaster, engineer, et al.). Each division would have a number, and many times also a nickname. The units assembled by Pershing, the 16th, 18th, 26th, and 28th regiments, together with the 6th Field Artillery, would be the nucleus of the 1st Division, the "Big Red One." Until that time, incredibly, no actual division had existed in the American Army.

As he assembled what would become the nucleus of an American Expeditionary Force (the AEF), Pershing was summoned to Washington to meet with Secretary of War Baker. Many considered the small, timid-looking Newton D. Baker an unlikely choice for such a vital position. Baker, however, a former student of Wilson's at Johns Hopkins, was a man of strong character and brilliant mind; he would prove to be one of America's finest secretaries of war [2-19].

Baker told Pershing he should take his provisional task force to France as soon as it was ready. Two days later, however, Baker told him his orders had been changed. He would not be commanding that newly formed division. For political purposes, as well as morale, it had become necessary to establish an American presence overseas, and soon. Pershing would now be going overseas at once as commander-in-chief of *all* American forces in Europe.

That afternoon, when Pershing met with Baker and President Wilson, Pershing was told his role was being expanded, mainly as a reaction to the Allied Military Missions now in Wash-

2-14 Troops playing baseball.

2-15 Drill sergeant overseeing fatigued Marines.

2-16 Marines practicing drill. Note dog leading the troops.

2-17, 2-18 Troops practicing marksmanship.

ington, a French group headed by Marshal Joffre and a British team led by Foreign Minister Arthur Balfour [2-20], Lloyd George's foreign secretary. Somewhat naively, Wilson had hoped America would be asked to furnish mainly shipping and war materiel. Now the Allies were telling him they mostly needed "men, men, men." It didn't matter if the men were trained: the Allies would do that when the troops arrived in France. Further, they needn't be in American divisions, as they could be fed into existing French and British units, which after the past three years were badly drained of manpower. What they needed most, according to General Robert-Georges Nivelle [2-21], Joffre's replacement, were thousands of laborers, railroad workers, drivers, stevedores, nurses, and doctors, so as to free more Frenchmen for battle.

Wilson knew full well that the American people would support neither the French nor the British plan, and for him personally it would be political suicide. Also, when the war was over, Wilson knew he would want to take his place at the head of the peace table, and the only way he could do that would be for American units to have a major *fighting* role in securing that peace.

For his chief-of-staff, Pershing selected General James G. Harbord. On May 19, Pershing, Harbord, and their headquarters staff sailed for Europe on the *USS Baltic*. Pershing's orders read:

> In military operations against the Imperial German Government, you are directed to cooperate with the forces of the other countries employed against that enemy; but in so doing the underlying idea must be kept in view that the forces of the United States are a separate and distinct component of the combined forces, the identity of which must be preserved.

Pershing landed in Liverpool, England, and, along with his

2-19 Secretary of War Newton D. Baker.

2-20 Arthur Balfour, Britain's foreign minister (1916–1922).

staff, boarded a train to London. As Pershing stepped from the train, American reporter Heywood Hale Broun thought, "No man ever looked more the ordained leader of fighting men." The British seemed overjoyed to finally see an American presence. Pershing met King George V, David Lloyd George, General Sir John French, South African General Jan Smuts [2-22], and numerous other dignitaries.

Then it was off to France, where the greetings were also enthusiastic. In Paris Pershing and a contingent from the 1st Division were greeted by cheering crowds that threw flowers and shouted "Vive l'Amerique!" [2-23 to 2-25].

Shortly after Pershing and his staff arrived in France, Pershing met with the new French commander-in-chief, the veteran Marshal Henri Petain [2-26], who had succeeded Nivelle. Earlier, Nivelle had replaced Joffre in that position; then, after the 1917 "Nivelle offensive" proved a dismal failure, Petain had been given the task of rebuilding the strength and esprit of the French Army.

Pershing and Petain met for the first time at the French GHQ at Compiegne. They eventually formed a liking for each other, perhaps because they were much alike—each man was pragmatic, blunt spoken, and stubborn. After the war, Pershing would say publicly that Petain was "the greatest general of the war." Although Petain obviously welcomed the American presence, he was realistic, commenting dolefully to Pershing, "I just hope it is not too late."

By June 1917, heavy casualties and a series of wasteful offensives had brought French morale to its lowest point yet; some units had even mutinied, refusing to return to the trenches. Petain took hold with a firm hand, determined to suppress the mutiny, punishing as few as possible, yet being merciless when needed. In all, 3,427 sentences were decreed, representing 10 percent of the mutineers. Of these, 554 were condemned to death, but only 49 were executed.

A remarkable scene took place on American Independence Day, July 4, 1917, when Pershing, accompanied by Mar-

2-21 General Nivelle.

shal Joffre and the French Minister of War M. Painleve, visited the tomb of Lafayette at Picpus Cemetery [2-27]. There Pershing delegated one of his staff, Captain Charles Stanton, to make some appropriate remarks. (Pershing's own French was serviceable but limited.) Stanton rose to the occasion, uttering the stirring words, "Lafayette, we are here!" Parisians went wild. Some reporters attributed the

2-22 General Jan Smuts.

2-23, 2-24, 2-25 1st Division greeted by cheering French crowds who are very happy to see American reinforcements.

2-26 General Petain, the hero of Verdun. Pershing found him to be the most congenial of the senior French commanders.

phrase to Pershing, and so, as Pershing's, it passed into American and French folklore. It was first suggested that Pershing use the phrase, and later he wished he had. At the time, though, while he agreed to Stanton's using it, he thought that coming from him, it would be "uncharacteristic."

Earlier that day, the 1st Division's 16th Infantry Regiment had paraded through Paris. Again it was an occasion for cheers. Everyone was expecting great things from the Yanks, and the *New York Times* proudly stated, "American Troops in First-Class Form for Fighting Land on French Soil."

The average American, however, like the average Frenchman, did not realize how little America was able to do at this point. Military men weren't so easily fooled. As they paraded in Paris, the Yanks looked like just what they were—untrained civilians wearing ill-fitting uniforms and having a hard time keeping in step. One French veteran turned to his companion in the crowd and said, "And they send *that* to help us!" [2-28]. Nevertheless, the overall effect was one of elation.

Winston Churchill would later write, "The impression made upon the hard-pressed French by this seemingly inexhaustible flood of gleaming youth in its first maturity of health and vigor was prodigious. . . . Half trained, half organized, with only their courage and their numbers and their magnificent youth behind their weapons, they were to buy their experience at a bitter price. But this they were quite ready to do."

2-27 Left to right: French Minister of War Painleve, General Pershing, and Marshal Joffre visiting the grave of Lafayette at Picpus.

2-28 American soldiers march by a Frenchman with a bicycle.

THREE

The War at Sea

The War at Sea

In August 1916, Congress au-thorized the construction of 157 warships. Secretary of the Navy Josephus Daniels [3-1], a former North Carolina news-paper editor, proclaimed it "the biggest shipbuilding program ever undertaken by any navy at any one time." Daniels, ironically, like Secretary of War Baker, was a former pacifist. Nevertheless, thanks in large part to Daniels and his assistant secretary, Franklin D. Roosevelt [3-2], the Navy, unlike the Army, was off to a good start in preparing for war. Others responsible, such as the House Naval Affairs Committee, took justifiable pride in what was be-ing accomplished [3-3].

The building program included battleships [3-4, 3-5], cruisers [3-6, 3-7], gunboats [3-8], destroyers, submarines [3-9, 3-10], torpedo boats [3-11, 3-12], and various other vessels, from fuel and supply ships to admirals' barges [3-13 to 3-15]. The major emphasis, however, was on the battleships and cruisers. This was

3-1 Secretary of the Navy Josephus Daniels.

3-2 Assistant Secretary of the Navy Franklin D. Roosevelt (left).

3-3 The House Naval Affairs Committee aboard the USS *Queenstown*.

3-4 The battleship USS *Louisiana*.

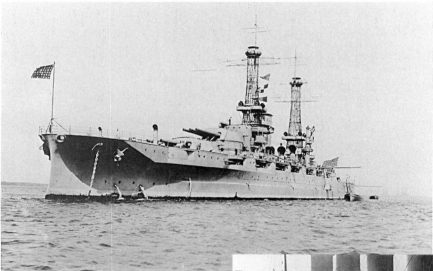

3-5 The battleship USS *Arizona*.

firepower. This was the highly publicized HMS *Dreadnought* [3-16]. Eventually the term "dreadnought" came into general usage, applied to all the mighty class of battleships coming into the German and British fleets.

Germany's Kaiser Wilhelm, however, who fancied himself as something of a naval figure [3-17], was also determined to have a powerful fleet, even declaring he wanted his German Navy to become as potent a force as the German Army. Some of this may have stemmed from Wilhelm's long-time respect for the Royal Navy, which was very sincere, as was his affection for his British relatives, particularly the one he called his "dear grandmama," Queen Victoria. (In 1901, when Victoria lay on her deathbed, Wilhelm was

understandable, since most people believed the Great War's decisive naval battles would be fought between the mighty battleships and their accompanying heavy cruisers.

Britain, the island nation, had dominated the seas for centuries. In recent years, moreover, it had increased its fleet by adding powerful vessels of war, perhaps the most famous being an extremely large, heavily armored battleship with impressive

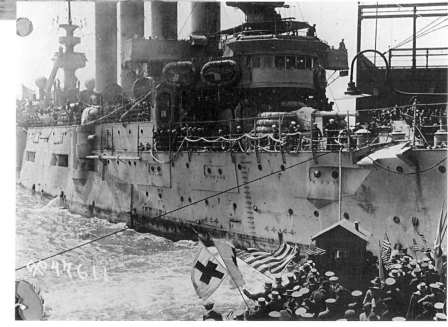

3-6 The USS *Charleston*, a cruiser.

3-7 The cruiser USS *Pueblo*.

3-8 The gunboat USS *Essex*.

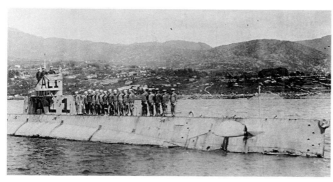

3-9 US Submarine 284.

3-10 US Submarine *Tarpon*.

3-11 Torpedo boat USS *Bainbridge*.

3-12 Torpedo boat USS *Blakely*.

3-13 Fuel ship USS *Ajax*.

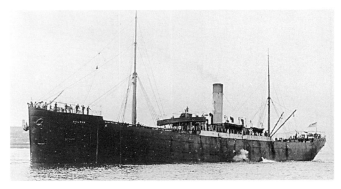

3-14 Supply ship USS *Celtic*.

3-15 "The Admiral's Barge" belonging to the USS *Mayflower*.

3-16 HMS *Dreadnought*.

3-17 Kaiser Wilhelm II at Kiel.

present alongside his uncle, the Prince of Wales. Once the Prince became King Edward VII, he returned the affection by impulsively making the Kaiser an honorary Field Marshal in the British Army.)

Soon, however, Wilhelm felt the conflict between his British family ties and his role as German Kaiser. He became determined not only to develop a mighty high seas fleet, but to make it one rivaling that of Britain's. What followed was a massive shipbuilding program, and by 1914 the German Navy took justifiable pride in its heavily armed battleships, cruisers,

and supporting craft, some lurking in port, others prowling the seas, and all ready to do battle [3-18 to 3-20].

3-18 German battleship *Geschnrader* (left) and other German warships in the North Sea.

3-19 German battleship *Deutschland.*

3-20 German battleship *Schleswig-Holstein.*

3-21 Admiral Jellicoe of the British Royal Navy.

3-22 Admiral von Scheer of the German Navy.

The climax came at the Battle of Jutland when, in the third year of the war, British and German fleets collided over a two-day period, May 31–June 1, 1916. The British fleet, under Admiral Sir John Jellicoe [3-21], had twenty-eight dreadnoughts and nine battle cruisers; the German, led by Admiral von Scheer [3-22], countered with sixteen dreadnoughts and five battle cruisers. The Germans could have claimed victory, since they lost fewer ships than did the British. At the decisive moment, however, von Scheer decided he

3-23 German submarines U-103, U-108, and U-113.

3-24 German submarine *Deutschland Bremen.*

3-25 German submarine U-14.

must save his remaining ships. The German fleet withdrew, falling back to its North Sea ports. Henceforth the two fleets would cancel each other out. The Germans, realizing they could not afford to fight another such battle, decided to concentrate on building submarines. Henceforth the most feared German ship of World War I would be the U-boat rather than the battleship [3-23 to 3-25].

As late as 1915, Admiral George Dewey, the "hero of Manila Bay" [3-26], had downgraded the submarine's importance. "The submarine is not an instrument fitted to dominate naval warfare," Dewey wrote. "The battleship is still the principal reliance of navies, as it has been in the past." He would soon be proven wrong. Once the Kaiser authorized unrestricted submarine warfare, and the U-boat captains were turned loose, they proceeded to wreak havoc with Allied shipping.

President Wilson recognized the U-boat threat and saw the importance of active collaboration between the U.S. and British Navies. He pulled from retirement a longtime Anglophile, the distinguished Admiral William Sowden Sims [3-27], who became the U.S. naval representative in Europe. In 1910, Sims, obviously exceeding his authority, had given a talk at the Guildhall in London in which he said, "If the time ever comes when the British Empire is seriously menaced by an external enemy, it is my opinion that you may count on upon every man, every dollar, every drop of blood, of your kindred across the sea." Navy Secretary Daniels was blunt when Sims was appointed to the European post: "You have been selected for this mission not because of your Guildhall speech, but in spite of it."

Sims arrived in London on April 9, 1917, by which time the U.S. had entered the war. Next day he met with British Admiral Sir John Jellicoe, who by that time had been named First Sea Lord. Jellicoe shocked

3-26 Admiral George Dewey.

3-27 Admiral William Sims.

3-28 HMS *Vindictive* sunk off the coast of Belgium.

Sims by telling him that 844 Allied ships had been sunk in the first three months of unrestricted submarine warfare [3-28 to 3-30]. The situation had become so bad that many sailors and merchant seamen were actually refusing to sail.

Both men agreed that at the moment Germany was winning. "It is impossible," Jellicoe said, "to go on with the war if losses like this continue." Dealing with the U-boat menace had to be given the highest priority. Sims recommended, and Lloyd George agreed, that a convoy system should be established whereby merchant ships, and later troop ships, would travel together and be accompanied by destroyers. The Admiralty was opposed, saying it would just be a waste of cruisers and destroyers. The Americans proposed laying a mine barrier across the North Sea and the English Channel. The Admiralty also

rejected that idea, calling it "quite unfeasible."

That summer, in frustration, Woodrow Wilson, addressing a group of naval officers from the quarterdeck of the USS *Pennsylvania* [3-31], urged them to ignore the Royal Navy and "throw caution to the winds." "Every time we have suggested anything to the British Admiralty," he said, "the reply has come back that virtually amounted to this, that it has never been done that way, and I

felt like saying, 'Well, nothing was ever done so systematically as nothing is being done now.' Therefore I should like to see something unusual happen. . . ."

President Wilson by this time knew the U-boat problem existed not only in the mid-Atlantic, but even along America's east coast. The civilian population was apprehensive, especially because of the frightening rumors that arose. Some of the rumors were authentic, but more often they bordered

3-29 The hospital ship *Gloucester Castle* sinking in the Mediterranean.

3-30 A German submarine torpedoing British ships in the North Sea.

3-31 USS *Pennsylvania.*

on the absurd. Some said that U-boats were landing spies or men to poison wells. Also, if a light flashed from shore, it was said to be a signal to a lurking German sub. One story even claimed that U-boats planned to launch airplanes to bomb New York City.

Some fears, however, turned into reality. Soon after the war started, one U-boat appeared off the New Jersey coast and proceeded to sink six ships. One of these, the passenger steamer *Carolina*, en route from Puerto Rico to New York, carried 218 passengers and a crew of 117. All aboard managed to make their way into lifeboats, but thirteen people lost their lives when one of the lifeboats capsized during a storm. Within twenty-four hours the Navy Department was besieged by anxious friends and relatives of those on board. In addition, some 5,000 telegrams, cables, and phone calls poured in, as Navy Secretary Daniels tried, with limited success, to answer reporters' shouted questions and calm civilian fears.

For Woodrow Wilson, the primary concern at the moment was getting members of the AEF safely to France. In the summer of 1917, the country was giving enthusiastic support to the war effort. Nevertheless, Wilson knew the sinking of a single troopship, along with the resulting heavy loss of life, would have a devastating effect on American morale.

FOUR

Getting the Boys "Over There"

Getting the Boys "Over There"

When Pershing and his staff sailed for Europe on the USS *Baltic*, they were accompanied by men from the 1st Division, the first American troops to land in France. Because of all the recent ship sinkings, there had been a certain amount of apprehension before the sailing. Fortunately, however, the crossing, which took ten days, proved uneventful. Until the *Baltic* reached the danger zone near Britain, it had traveled more or less straight along the North Atlantic sea lane. Then the ship began zigzagging, two destroyers arrived to act as escorts, and port was reached in good order. While the crossing had gone well, it was also chancy. It was decided that future troop crossings would rely on the newly established convoy system.

Early in the war, the British had tried keeping the sea lanes safe by means of patrols. Once the U-boat wolf packs began unrestricted hunting, the system had broken down, and the losses had been staggering. For three years the Admiralty had resisted introducing a convoy system, believing it unwise to see its warships taken away from the fleet and diverted from participation, however remote the possibility, in another major sea battle such as Jutland. But patrols had failed, and it was decided at least to give the convoy system a try. Henceforth ships crossing the Atlantic would travel in groups and be given naval protection.

The first convoy sailed on May 10, 1917. It proved an immediate success, with ship losses beginning to decrease dramatically. Only one ship (which had fallen behind from the group) was lost on that first convoy. The following month, June 1917, sixty merchant ships crossed in convoy without a single loss. Typically, some ten to fifty merchant ships, as well as one or more troop transports, traveled together and were escorted by a cruiser, a half-dozen destroyers, armed trawlers, and torpedo boats [4-1, 4-2].

There were of course significant disadvantages to the system. For example, a convoy had to travel at the speed of its slowest ship. Eventually, however, this was countered by organizing

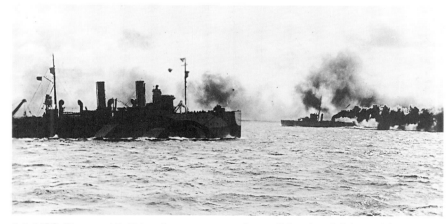

4-1 USS *Shawmut* (left) leading a convoy column, flying the division guide pennant and a submarine warning flag somewhere in the North Sea.

4-2 Destroyer guarding a transport in the North Sea.

4-3 The USS *Covington* sinking near the coast of France, July 1918.

slow-, medium-, and fast-speed convoys for greater efficiency. Another disadvantage was that convoys arrived en masse at the port, creating congestion.

In time, port facilities were expanded, and additional ports were made available. But when ships left the convoy to head for their respective ports, traveling individually or in small groups, they became particularly vulner-

able. Some, like the *Covington* [4-3], sunk almost within sight of land. In addition to the convoy system, an important development in antisubmarine warfare was the effective use of depth charges. Until 1916, there had been no way of sinking a submerged submarine. The depth charge, invented by the Royal Navy, changed that. A three-hundred-pound drum of

TNT with a variable water-pressure fuse, it could simply be rolled off the deck and into the water. A later development, this time an American invention, was the "Y gun," which allowed the drums to be hurled with greater accuracy and less risk [4-4]. Nevertheless, the submarine remained the principal threat on the high seas, with German raiders and torpedo

4-4 USS *Whipple* using "Y gun" to launch a 300-pound depth bomb while guarding a convoy in the North Sea.

4-5 The German raider *Alexandra Agassiz* being towed by a U.S. Navy ship.

boats playing only a limited role [4-5 to 4-7].

The summer of 1917 saw American troops heading for ports of embarkation in ever-increasing numbers [4-8]. Very few of the young soldiers had ever been away from their native state, let alone out of the country. To most of them, crossing the sea to a foreign land must have seemed a romantic adventure. Once they were aboard ship, however, the holiday atmosphere quickly evaporated. Many ships were so crowded that men had to sleep in shifts [4-9]. Food prepared in steaming, smelly galleys was a source of constant complaint. It was invariably overcooked, often of poor quality, and a far cry from the home cooking the young Yanks had known. Stormy seas and nervous stomachs made the situation even worse, and seasickness was all too common. One soldier wrote home that he had six meals a day—three down and three up. For those sailing on foreign ships, there was an added problem. One soldier wrote of the food on a British ship, "The steam-cooked unseasoned stuff—rice, meal, potatoes and tripe—prepared by English cooks in their native manner, was so unpalatable and sickening that I ate little during the voyage."

Whenever possible, the soldiers would leave the cramped sleeping areas to gather on deck, perhaps to gamble

4-6 German prisoners aboard a U.S. warship after being taken from the raider *Alexandra Agassiz*.

4-7 Unidentified German torpedo boats in the North Sea.

4-8 American troops on a train heading for their port of embarkation.

4-9 Crowded ship conditions for troops heading to Europe.

4-10 Soldiers passing time gambling.

4-11 Crewmen aboard ship.

[4-10], to visit with the crew (or a crew member's pet [4-11]) to scan the horizon looking for periscopes. Many a man spent hours trying to sight a U-boat periscope, or as one said, "trying to spot something I didn't ever want to see."

When a worldwide flu epidemic developed, the disease inevitably carried over to the troop ships. The overcrowding and poor sanitation compounded the problem, and in the months ahead, influenza proved more deadly than the U-boats. Isolation wards were created on board ship, often by converting space formerly used

4-12 A medical isolation ward aboard ship. This space was formerly used for cargo.

4-13 U.S. Marines coming alongside a port in France to be unloaded.

4-14 U.S. transports arriving at St. Nazaire, France.

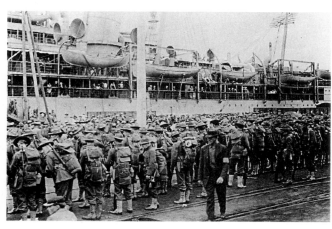

4-15 Marines disembarking in France.

for cargo storage [4-12]. During the war some 5,000 sailors, as well as many soldiers and marines, would die of respiratory diseases.

When ships docked and troops prepared to disembark, it was a happy moment all around [4-13]. The U-boat gauntlet had been run successfully, seasick stomachs could begin to recover, and the food on shore was *bound* to be better! Optimistic, enthusiastic young Americans were gladly trading the ship for the shore. Most men felt personally invulnerable, unwilling to consider the dangers that might lie ahead. The Navy saw the situation from a different perspective. William Halsey, who would win fame in the Pacific during World War II, was a captain of one of the escort destroyers. Halsey wrote in his diary, "You look at them [the troops], and pity them having to go to the trenches. Suppose they look at you and wonder why anyone is damn fool enough to roll and jump

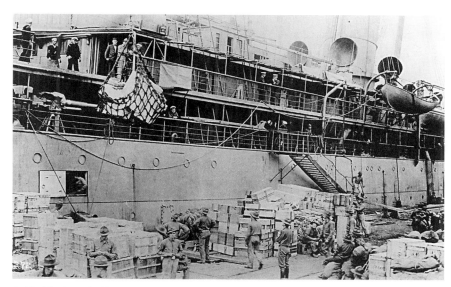

4-16 Marines in France unloading their transport.

4-17 U.S. soldiers working in a war garden.

4-18 An English woman working on a farm to help supply the British army.

4-19 German prisoners equipped with scythes and rakes marching to cut wheat on farms somewhere in France.

4-20 Mine layer USS *San Francisco*.

around on a destroyer." By late 1917, both troops and supplies were being unloaded in ever increasing numbers [4-14 to 4-16].

Convoys might be getting through, but shipping remained in short supply. Everything, including food, was now in a critical situation. In France and England, "war gardens" had been established to alleviate the situation [4-17 to 4-19]. England, said Jellicoe, was "in measurable distance of strangulation."

The U.S. Navy had provided most of the warships escorting the troop transports. The transports themselves, however, were mostly French or British. This was not a "freebie"; the United States was expected to pay for each man's passage. The cost had to be negotiated, especially when France initially tried to charge the same rate as for a prewar passenger liner. (After some hard bargaining, the per capita cost was reduced.)

Allocating ships became a question of priority, and, almost inevitably, disputes arose. The British, for example, relied on cargo ships for their very survival and were reluctant to allocate shipping to America. At the same time, the British insisted that the Yanks increase the flow of troops to Europe. The Americans, in turn, argued that if the British wanted more troops to sail, they should be willing to provide more shipping space. Winston Churchill agreed. Churchill, a lifelong advocate of Anglo-American cooperation,

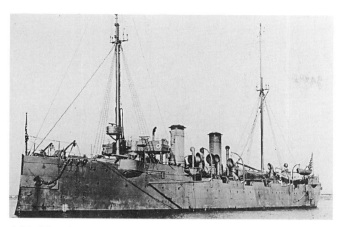

4-21 Mine layer USS *Baltimore.*

4-22 An unknown mine layer somewhere in the Atlantic.

4-23 USN 404, a fleet of mines in the North Sea.

4-24 Mines aboard the USS *San Francisco.*

4-25 Poster urging men to join the famous Fighting 69th Irish Regiment.

4-26 Poster urging American men to join the Air Service.

4-27 Poster urging men to join the Army.

4-28 Men being urged to finish Liberty Destroyer 139.

4-29 Builders who worked on Liberty Destroyer 139.

told his countrymen that the Royal Navy and the Mercantile Marine should devote more effort to the transporting of American troops. The question was not only military, but also political. "Quite apart from the imperious military need," Churchill told the War Cabinet in March of 1918, "the intermingling of British and American units on the field of battle and their endurance of losses and suffering together may exert an immeasurable effect upon the future destiny of the English-speaking peoples, and will afford us perhaps the only guarantee of safety if Germany emerges stronger from the war than she entered it."

When the war began in 1914, many German ships had headed to neutral American ports. Once America entered the war, these ships were confiscated and put to Allied use. One such vessel, the *Vaterland*, was the second largest ship afloat. Having been

renamed *Leviathan*, it became the fastest and largest of all troop transports. Eventually it would carry thousands of Americans, both to the war and, once peace was secured, back home again.

Later in the war, a major factor in countering the U-boat menace was the erection of a mine barrier across the North Sea and the English Channel. British and

American ships called "mine planters" went into action and began laying the first mines in June 1918 [4-20 to 4-22]. The mines, stretching across the Straits of Dover and all the way from Scotland to the coast of Norway, slammed the door on U-boat access to the Atlantic, though the number of U-boats sunk by the mine barrier was unknown. In the opinion of Navy

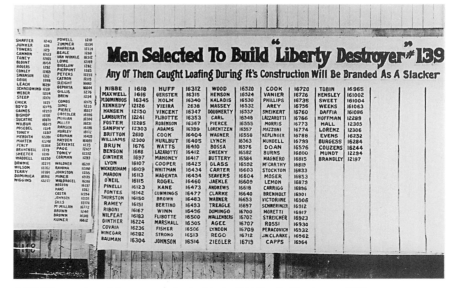

4-30 The roster of the men selected to build Liberty Destroyer 139.

4-31 The Liberty Destroyer *Santa Ana* in port after its launch.

4-32 A merchant marine ship being built.

4-33 Workers with a sign over their heads reading "Thirty days or bust."

Secretary Daniels, "there was no one thing that had more influence in breaking the German morale, particularly in the U-boat service, than did the Northern Mine Barrage." Even Admiral Sims, who was first skeptical about the project, called it "one of the wonders of the war" [4-23, 4-24].

Meanwhile at home, patriotic Americans were supporting the war effort with enthusiasm. Recruiting posters were everywhere urging young men to get in uniform [4-25 to 4-27]. Shipyards were turning out new warships in record time [4-28 to 4-31] as well as making a maximum effort to rebuild a merchant fleet that had been crippled by U-boat losses [4-32, 4-33]. Without the clearance of the sea lanes and the eventual defeat of the German submarines, however, the men and materials so dearly needed from the United States may never have gotten to Europe, and the final outcome of the war may have been entirely different.

FIVE

Training in France

Training in France

They were mostly called "Yanks," especially by the Europeans. Somewhere along the way, however, both at home and among the troops themselves, the name "Doughboy" became popular. They began arriving in France throughout the summer of 1917, although not in the numbers the British and French would have liked. The American 1st and 2nd Divisions were the first sizeable units to land. They were supposedly part of the regular army, but that was mostly in name. In truth, most members were raw recruits with less than a year's service, unfortunately not up to speed in either training or equipment. A distinctive feature of the 2nd Division was that it contained both Army and Marines. Even the high-spirited Marines, however, were far from combat-ready as they arrived at the French port of St. Nazaire [5-1, 5-2].

In late September, the U.S. 26th Division also began to disembark, although the full division wouldn't be on hand until the beginning of 1918. The 26th,

5-1 Marines arriving at St. Nazaire, France.

5-2 Marines aboard ship.

5-3 Colonel Douglas MacArthur.

a National Guard unit originally from New England, was popularly known as the "Yankee Division." It contained several men who had seen service with Pershing in Mexico as well as many skilled mechanics and office men who were "acquaintances and friends." Although a large percentage of the unit was made up of volunteers, the ranks had been brought up to strength by the addition of conscripts. Oddly enough, although the 26th was commanded by a West Pointer, Major General Clarence R. Edwards, it had the reputation of being generally contemptuous of the regular army. Pershing attributed much of this to the Yankee Division's commander. In Pershing's opinion, which was shared by many other regular officers, Edwards had adopted too

many "National Guard ways" and had allowed a spirit of elitism to develop throughout his unit. A mutual animosity developed between Pershing and Edwards, and the situation was made worse by Edwards's sharp tongue and sarcastic remarks, which were usually directed toward higher headquarters. As long as Edwards did the job, however, Pershing managed to keep his resentment in check.

As it turned out, the 26th would become one of the most active American divisions, amassing more days at the front (205) than any other except the 1st Division (228), and spending 45 days in battle, more than the 1st, which would have 28. By war's end, the 26th Division would have fought in seven major engagements and taken some 3,000 prisoners.

In October, following close behind the 26th, was another National Guard unit, the U.S. 42nd Division, which also profited from having a number of men in its ranks who had served in 1916 with Pershing's Mexican expedition. The 42nd was initially commanded by the elder General William Mann, West Point class of 1886. Two months later he would be replaced by the younger Major General Charles Menoher, an able soldier and a team builder. The team in this case, assembled in France, was a collection of National Guard units from twenty-six different states. Cobbling such a unit together had strong political im-

plications. For months, various governors had been insisting that some of their own state guardsmen should be utilized at the earliest opportunity. In response, nearly everyone was allowed to get in the act. Remarkably enough, the idea worked. At a press conference, the 42nd's chief-of-staff, Colonel Douglas MacArthur [5-3], compared the division's structure to a rainbow spanning the country. Thereupon a reporter called it the "Rainbow Division," and the name stuck.

From his first days with the 42nd, the flamboyant MacArthur was making a name for himself. Even before the 42nd itself went on line, MacArthur, disdaining to wear a helmet or carry a gas

5-4 General James Harbord.

mask, accompanied French troops on a trench raid, armed only with a trench knife and a riding crop. After savage fighting, the party returned at daybreak escorting a large number of German prisoners. Frenchmen crowded around the American colonel, shaking his hand, slapping him on the back, offering him cognac and absinthe. Later, French General Baudelaire, after kissing MacArthur on both cheeks, pinned a Croix de Guerre on his chest.

General Menoher, to his credit, did not seem to mind being overshadowed by his publicity conscious chief-of-staff and would tell a *New York Times* reporter, "Colonel MacArthur is one of the ablest officers in the United States Army and one of the most popular." There was a different reaction to MacArthur among the staff officers at AEF headquarters, particularly after MacArthur protested an order that would have assigned thirty-three of the 42nd Division's officers to other units. He sent a strongly worded, anguished wire to high-level friends in Washington, urging them to intervene. In response, pressure mounted, and, armed with stateside political support, MacArthur went to Pershing's chief-of-staff, James Harbord [5-4]. Eventually Harbord convinced Pershing to rescind the order, but it was the sort of episode people didn't forget.

Despite the Yanks' scarcity in numbers, they had all been cheered on their arrival, whether

5-5 French citizens watch a parade of Yanks march through town.

at the port [5-5] or in the streets of Paris. In the 1st Division's parade on the 4th of July, they had even been escorted by a French military band [5-6]. Now it was time to depart the ports, leave the lights of Paris, and get to work at serious training. In the week following the parade, Americans began moving to a spot near Gondrecourt, a village in Lorraine about sixty miles south of Verdun and an area that afforded ample room for training and setting up camps. The rail movement was by

5-6 A parade featuring a French military band.

5-7 U.S. Marines in railcars on their way to assignment.

means of the infamous "40 and 8's," the crude "Quarante hommes ou huit chevaux" box-cars designed to carry either forty men or eight horses [5-7].

At the new training area, some men were billeted in civilian homes and some bedded down in barns that they joked were also "40 and 8's," meaning forty men in the loft, eight horses on the ground floor. Others went into empty French barracks that they found appalling.

Back in the States, they had lived in temporary structures put together with wartime haste. But at least those barracks were clean, and with flush toilets. The new buildings were not only filthy, but the toilet "facility" was a mere hole in the floor. However, the civilians were friendly, and their new Yankee neighbors were duly appreciative [5-8].

In July, Pershing slipped away from Paris to accept a long-standing invitation to visit the British Expeditionary Force (BEF). Accompanied by James Harbord, his chief-of-staff, and Lieutenant George Patton, his aide, Pershing drove to St. Omer, about twenty miles south of Dunkirk, where Field Marshal Sir Douglas Haig kept his personal command post in a picturesque old chateau [5-9]. Haig greeted his American counterpart cordially and took an immediate liking to Pershing, whose formal, dignified manner was something Haig had not expected in an American. Their conversation went well, although it became obvious that Haig's primary interest was in how soon the Americans would be on line and ready to fight. Pershing, who knew he had a long training task ahead, could offer nothing specific about a timetable and was forced to remain noncommittal.

On the other hand, Pershing

5-8 Schoolchildren welcoming U.S. Marines.

5-9 Field Marshal Sir Douglas Haig.

5-10 Prime Minister David Lloyd George.

5-11 An American encampment of pup tents.

learned all he could about the British situation, especially after he and Haig were joined by General Sir William Robertson, Chief of the Imperial General Staff. Haig and Robertson were quite frank, admitting that they had lost some 175,000 men in their recent offensive at Arras. Pershing offered no criticism, but he was shocked by what he considered a costly, ill-advised war of attrition.

Next, soon after he returned to Paris, Pershing accepted a breakfast invitation from David Lloyd George, the British Prime Minister [5-10]. Although Pershing was probably unaware of it, Lloyd George had suffered politically because of the shocking British losses and was probably the most severe critic of Haig's and Robertson's tactics. His conversation with Pershing, however, dealt with political matters, notably his concern about their ally Russia, which he feared would soon be out of the war. Once again Pershing, who limited his opinions to military matters and shied away from politics, was forced to remain noncommittal.

As training got under way near Gondrecourt, camps were being organized. Cities with two-man "pup tents" sprung up [5-11], and in many places army engineers were soon erecting new wooden barracks [5-12]. In addition, kitchens started operating. As in every war throughout history, soldiers often griped about the "chow" even as they

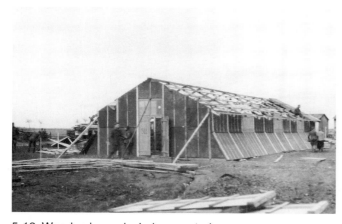

5-12 Wooden barracks being erected.

5-13 The 16th Infantry Regiment's camp kitchen.

5-14 Soldiers waiting for food at the mess tent.

5-15 Soldiers stringing cable over railroad tracks.

tic difficulties right from the start. Before long, Pershing asked the War Department to send a hundred telephone operators fluent in French. These women would not be assigned to combat units, Pershing said, but they "will do as much to help win the war as the men in khaki." Additional telephone lines were also needed, and the Army Signal Corps began installing miles of new pole lines and leasing other lines from the French. By the end of the war they would have leased 12,000 miles of wire from the French and laid 22,000 miles of new wire [5-15].

In Pershing's opinion, a distinct advantage of the move was his ability to escape the distractions of Paris. In the fabulous "City of Light," he and his staff had been constantly wined and dined, perhaps too

5-16 Charles Dawes, head of the General Purchasing Board.

consumed it in prodigious quantities [5-13, 5-14].

By September, Pershing was also moving his headquarters to Chaumont, a town of about 20,000 at the confluence of the Marne and the Suize, not far from the front. Pershing and Harbord decided it was an ideal location. It was served by a major railroad line on the planned artery between St. Nazaire and Verdun. Also, there was a large public building in the center of

town, ideal for a major headquarters. Soon the name "Chaumont" became synonymous with Headquarters AEF.

Getting operating, however, required more than a bit of doing, and a major priority was the establishment of a communications system by improving the antiquated French telephone system and training the people who would use it. Coping with the French operators posed linguis-

much so. While they were grateful, this wasn't the reason the AEF had come to France. Moreover, even as the Allies were welcoming them, it was obvious that the French and British, veterans now of three years of bloody war, were skeptical about the Americans' military know-how. In Paris, a French general, referring to the officers with Pershing, had asked, "Is this your personal staff?"

"No," said Pershing, "it is my General Staff."

The general persisted, insisting that it took thirty years to build a competent General Staff.

"It never took Americans thirty years to do anything!" Pershing snapped back.

At Chaumont, Pershing and his officers got down to business, planning the difficult training tasks that lay ahead. Equally important was organizing the logistical support structure. How would supplies arrive? What were the available port facilities? How would critical items be allocated and delivered into the hands of troops? There were countless decisions to be made, decisions for which there was no precedent. Pershing faced up to them, taking several courageous, innovative actions. On his own initiative, for example, he contracted with the French government for 5,000 planes at a cost of $60 million, more than Congress had appropriated initially for the entire Spanish-American War. "It was no time

5-17 British instructor giving lessons to GI's on the use of grenades.

to discuss technicalities," Pershing said later.

At this point the number of Americans in Europe was comparatively small. However, it was obvious that the Doughboys would soon be arriving in overwhelming numbers, with an immediate need for proper tools, weapons, clothing, and

equipment. So far elements of the AEF had been purchasing needed items directly from the French and British, with various headquarters actually competing with each other. Once again on his own initiative, Pershing set up a General Purchasing Board (GPB), comprised of ten AEF officers, plus YMCA and Red

5-18 Highland instructors.

5-19 Group of French tank officers and crews instructing Americans on tank warfare.

5-20 Americans being trained to throw grenades.

5-21 Another group of Americans being trained to throw grenades.

Cross representatives. Its mission was to centralize and distribute needed items, obtaining as much as possible from European sources and thereby freeing shipping space for the movement of troops. Oddly enough, after three years of war, neither of the Allied armies had established anything similar to the GPB, which meant at this stage that the Americans had no one point of contact when they wished to obtain supplies and equipment. They were on their own as they tried to locate horses, fodder, mechanical transport, medical supplies, food, coal, and all the other things needed to sustain an army in the field.

Pershing named Charles G. Dawes [5-16], a successful businessman and an old friend from University of Nebraska days, to run the GPB. Dawes, in Pershing's words "the most unmilitary human who ever lived," who later became U.S. vice president under Calvin Coolidge, combined drive and business acumen to make the GPB highly effective.

Ultimately over twenty different training schools were set up, with classes led by American officers and noncoms, often with the help of French and British instructors [5-17 to 5-19]. In many ways it was a "bootstrap" operation, with American instructors teaching things they had just learned themselves. Mostly they concentrated on the basic combat skills of a soldier, such as throwing hand grenades [5-20, 5-21],

5-22 Bayonet practice.

5-23 Practicing a French method of using the bayonet.

5-24 GI's receiving machine gun instruction.

or drilling with the bayonet [5-22, 5-23]. A few, however, had to learn the use of automatic weapons [5-24], or acquire skills such as the rigging of telephone lines [5-25], digging trenches for protection against air raids, or purifying water [5-26, 5-27]. Physical fitness was also emphasized, both calisthenics, of which most men took a dim view [5-28 to 5-30], and sports such as

5-25 GI rigging telephone line.

5-26 Americans digging trenches near Hermitage, France.

5-27 Soldiers filling canteens with purified water.

5-28 Soldiers removing outer garments for physical training.

the winners. The ubiquitous General Pershing, always on the move, sometimes even made an appearance, to observe or give out trophies [5-37, 5-38]. "Black Jack" Pershing wasn't just observing athletic contests or parades, of course. This was a time of evaluation, for every leader, from corporal to general. Those who showed promise would be given increased responsibilities; those who didn't measure up would be weeded out. Ruthlessly.

baseball, boxing, or rough and tumble "cockfights," which were much more popular [5-31 to 5-34]. In addition, the drill and ceremonies that helped convert citizens into soldiers was also made part of the training regime [5-35, 5-36].

As a morale booster, field days were also held, with prizes for

The most popular event for the troops was "pay day," though it necessitated Americans becoming acquainted with

5-29, 5-30 Soldiers preparing for a three-legged race training exercise.

5-31, 5-32 Soldiers playing baseball.

5-33 Boxing match.

5-34 Cockfighting.

strange-looking French currency [5-39 to 5-42].

The "Big Red One" 1st Division spent the last two weeks in July training with a battalion from an elite French division, the Chasseurs Alpins, known as the Blue Devils [5-43]. These were veterans with wide-ranging experience, and the Americans paid respectful attention. The 1st Division's operations officer, George C. Marshall [5-44], spoke of the Blue Devils as "picked fellows of an unusually

5-35 16th Infantry field training.

5-36 Color guard, 16th Infantry.

5-37 Trophies and prizes waiting to be awarded.

5-38 General Pershing awarding trophies at field day.

5-39 The pay tent.

5-40 Pay day for the 5th Marines.

5-41 A soldier trying to count his French Francs.

vigorous type . . . with a magnificent fighting record." Marshall, of course, would become world famous during World War II as the Army's chief-of-staff. Other 1st Division members who would rise to prominence included Peyton March, who in 1918 would be elevated to Army chief-of-staff in Washington; Charles Sommerall [5-45], a future division and corps commander; Hanson Ely, later to lead the 5th Division [5-46]; and Frank Parker [5-47], who would also rise to become one of the 1st Division's commanders.

Much as they respected the Blue Devils and others who came to teach and share their experiences, the Americans disagreed when it came to the use of rifles. The Allied officers, teaching trench warfare, told the Yanks to forget about using their rifles. The most important skill, they said, was knowing how to duck into a shell hole, peep over the top, lob a grenade, then scuttle back a few yards to one's own trenches. This was not what the aggressive Yanks wanted to hear, nor was it in keeping with Pershing's emphasis on rifle

5-42 Soldiers gambling their money away ten minutes after collecting their pay.

5-43 Group of French Chasseurs Alpins instructors in Gondrecourt, France.

5-44 George C. Marshall.

5-45 Charles Summerall.

5-46 Colonel Hanson Ely.

marksmanship [5-48], accompanied by fire and movement. Pershing believed that "victory could not be won by the costly process of attrition, but must be won by driving the enemy out into the open and engaging him in a war of movement."

Major General Robert Lee

Bullard [5-49], who had served with Pershing in the Philippines, also deplored the French tactics. "A French soldier never rests," said the outspoken Bullard, "until he has dug a hole, and after that he never rests anywhere than in the hole."

Meanwhile the Allies, particu-

larly the French, became increasingly frustrated by what they considered American procrastination. They didn't care about state of training—they wanted to see Doughboys in the trenches! In a way it was understandable. Earlier, French General Robert Nivelle (who had succeeded

5-47 Frank Parker.

5-48 Target training.

5-49 Major General Robert Lee Bullard.

Joffre as commander-in-chief of French armies North and Northeast) has launched a major offensive, predicting it would "break the German front." The offensive had but limited success, and the main result was even more casualties and a weakening of French army morale. In the weeks that followed, some French units would refuse to march; a few would actually mutiny. As a consequence, General Henri-Philippe Petain was named to replace Nivelle and given the job of rebuilding the army and restoring morale. It was an overwhelming task. To the French commanders, and the French people, the complete fall of France seemed all too possible.

French Prime Minister Georges Clemenceau said as much in September 1917 when he visited the 1st Division, then under the command of General William Sibert, an officer who had won distinction as an engineer during the construction of the Panama Canal [5-50]. If they continued to procrastinate, Clemenceau told Sibert, Americans might end up "trying in vain to organize on lost battlefields over the graves of Allied soldiers." He didn't want to hear any more excuses as to why Americans were not arriving in France in large numbers, nor did he want to hear more talk of training needs. All he wanted, Clemenceau said, was for American soldiers, regardless of their condition, to be sent as fast as possible to relieve the exhausted French armies. Clemenceau realized, and he hoped Sibert did as well, that there was also a significant psychological factor involved. French strength and morale were at an all-time low, and the appearance of Americans on line would at least give hope to the French people. America had been at war for nearly six

months, and still no Yank unit had been seen on the line. It might even be a question of winning or losing the war. In any event, it was time for the Yanks to show they were in earnest.

Sibert tried hard to present a counterargument. Both the Allies and the Germans were watching the 1st Division, thinking it represented the cream of America's regular army. In truth, however, it was full of new recruits, and they needed to be properly trained before they were sent into action. The argument made sense, but clearly Clemenceau and his generals weren't buying it.

"It was obviously quite out of place," Pershing said, "for Monsier Clemenceau to make any such demand, yet there is little doubt that he gave expression to a very general sentiment among the French people at that moment. They simply wanted to see American troops in the trenches."

5-50 General William Sibert

The pressure for Yank participation continued to mount, and most of it was directed toward Pershing. Even James Harbord, Pershing's loyal chief-of-staff, believed that his boss "risked the chance of being cursed to the latest generation, if through failure to cooperate, the war were to be lost."

Clemenceau and his generals came up with a plan to secure Yank participation, at least on a token, symbolic basis. They would have small American units, a battalion at a time, take their place on a quiet section of the line under French control. The plan was approved by Pershing, and at the beginning of October, an order arrived at 1st Division headquarters saying that one battalion from each of the division's four regiments would leave Gondrecourt and go onto line. They would be under the guidance of the French 18th Division, which was holding a six-mile sector about ten miles east of Nancy. As part of their combat indoctrination, each of these battalions would be "brigaded" with French troops. General Sibert and his division staff officers were to keep hands off; they were in fact forbidden even to visit the units once they left Gondrecourt.

Back in August 1917, Pershing had been disappointed when he inspected the 1st Division, finding it to be sloppy-looking and lacking in discipline. He was also unimpressed by Sibert. Nevertheless he chose the "Big Red One" to provide the first units to go on line. They began moving up on October 21, and for the first few days all went well. Things would soon change.

SIX

The Tools of War

The Tools of War

It has been said that war, like necessity, is the mother of invention. That was certainly true for World War I. Never before had so much innovation taken place so quickly, with changes not only in the methods of war but with the tools used to wage that war. Internal combustion engines, wireless telegraphy, breech loading rifles, machine guns, flame throwers, quick firing artillery, chemical weapons, smokeless powder—all were new to the battlefield. These innovations, plus the fact that the war was being fought overseas, brought tremendous logistical problems for the American Army.

The Doughboy himself carried a Springfield M-1903 rifle, usually called simply the "03." It was a superb weapon for its time and would, in fact, be standard equipment for an entire generation of American soldiers, being replaced only when the Garand M-1 came into production around the beginning of World War II [6-1, 6-2]. Unfortunately, not every

6-1 American soldiers in place with their Springfield rifles.

6-2 Men from the 18th Infantry Regiment cleaning their weapons.

Doughboy was armed with a Springfield, which was produced in only two factories, the Springfield Arsenal in Springfield, Massachusetts, and the Rock Island Arsenal at Rock Island, Illinois. By 1917, the latter would have ceased production of the Springfield. Some U.S. regular army units were equipped with Krag-Jorgenson rifles, which had been used in the Philippines against the Moros, but were now considered obsolete. When America entered the war, it had in its inventory about 600,000 Springfields, 160,000 Krags, and 40,000 sawed-off shotguns, the latter being used for close-in trench warfare or fighting in dense forests.

A bayonet for the Doughboy's rifle was also standard equipment. He normally carried it in a scabbard, but on special occasions, either for show or for close-quarter combat, he would attach it to the end of his weapon [6-3]. Although there were few actual bayonet fights during the war, it was comforting to have one available against a fortified enemy. Also, there was a psychological impact on a defender when an attack was launched with bayonets prominently displayed.

The Doughboy's "personal artillery" was the hand grenade, an ancient weapon that for some reason had fallen out of use prior to 1914. Oddly enough, at the beginning of the war the British had no grenades, even though the "British grenadier" was a storied

6-3 American soldier being accosted by a civilian. Note the bayonet on his rifle.

6-4 A soldier throwing a hand grenade.

individual and "grenadier regiments" still existed. Traditionally these were elite units of tall soldiers who were once specially trained to use these weapons effectively. For Germans, on the other hand, grenades were standard issue. When the British reintroduced grenades in France, the men who used them were called bombers. By the time America entered the

war, the grenade was considered an invaluable weapon for close combat and highly recommended by both the French and British. It would eventually be put to good use by the Americans [6-4, 6-5].

The Doughboy wore around his waist a web cartridge belt, with pouches containing spare ammunition clips for his weapon. On his legs were either the ungainly, awkward leather

6-5 Soldiers loading hand grenades.

leggings or the cumbersome wrap-around "puttees." On his head was a steel helmet of English design, a reminder of medieval times, and the first use of armor since its disappearance in the seventeenth century. Though the helmets were badly designed, the United States would buy 1.5 million of them from the British [6-6, 6-7]. German helmets, by contrast, were much better and similar to those worn by today's American army.

Despite their shortcomings, helmets at least offered more protection than the wide-brimmed Stetson "campaign hat," as worn by the officers in photo 6-8, or the cloth garrison hat, familiarly known as the "overseas cap" [6-9].

An infantryman marching to the front was also equipped with a canteen and a small shovel known as an entrenching tool. The pack on his back generally

contained mess gear, extra socks and underwear, toilet articles, and perhaps a blanket, plus miscellaneous personal items [6-10, 6-11]. Altogether, the Doughboy was burdened with a tremendous load: ten-pound rifle, bayonet,

entrenching tool, ammunition, and canteen, plus a large pack, added up to sixty to seventy pounds or more. A harness with strips of canvas webbing helped distribute weight as evenly as possible over the entire body; even so, there was a real strain on the shoulders and back.

Once he entered combat, the Doughboy would encounter ghastly weapons of sheer horror, ones that had been unknown in previous wars. There was the flame thrower (*Flammenwerfer*), first used by the French in the Argonne Forest in 1914 and later perfected by the Germans. It was a fearsome device offering instant cremation. In February 1915, the Germans used this weapon against French trenches near Verdun; this was the first of an estimated 650 flame thrower attacks. The trench system, how-

6-6 An American private wearing the poorly designed British-style helmet, which left the sides of the head exposed.

6-7 Soldier carrying a regulation pack.

6-8 Officers wearing Stetson campaign hats.

6-9 Officers wearing overseas caps.

6-10 U.S. 18th Infantry with full packs en route to the front.

6-11 Five soldiers displaying full packs of equipment.

ever, with its deep protection, gave flame throwers little more than the element of surprise and rendered them mostly ineffectual.

Then there were the poison gases, beginning with chlorine. In April 1915, the Germans introduced gas warfare with a surprise attack, discharging, within five minutes, 168 tons of chlorine from 4,000 cylinders against two French divisions. The effect was devastating, creating a huge gap in the line as troops fled in panic. They left behind, according to one report, hundreds of men in a "comatose or dying position." The Germans advanced cautiously, wearing respirators, and in short order had taken 2,000 prisoners and captured fifty-one guns. By the end of 1915 both sides were using even more lethal gases, such as phosgene, which asphyxiated, and mustard, a blistering agent [6-12].

The most effective weapon of "no man's land" was

6-12 Soldiers in gas masks go over the top.

6-13 Infantrymen ready to fire a machine gun. Note the soldier on his back feeding ammunition.

6-14 Officer talking to his machine gunners at the front.

6-15 Machine gun crew training.

undoubtedly the machine gun [6-13, 6-14]. At the beginning of the war, many senior officers viewed machine guns skeptically, believing they consumed ammunition at a too rapid, wasteful rate. Even a senior British general, Field Marshal Sir Douglas Haig, would consider them overrated, saying, "two per battalion is more than sufficient." The Germans, on the other hand, recognized the machine gun's potential, and began deploying them en masse early in the war. Their effectiveness was soon demonstrated. In

September 1915, twelve British battalions, about 10,000 men, left their trenches following a twenty-minute artillery barrage and "went over the top," as the expression went. Waiting for them were well-entrenched Germans, whose machine guns loosed a stream of bullets with deadly precision. Three and a half hours later, when the British staggered back to their lines, they left behind on the ground, or draped on the barbed wire, 385 officers and 7,861 other ranks. The Germans did not lose a single soldier.

The Allies learned the lesson. France had begun the war with only 2,500 machine guns; by war's end it had built and deployed some 314,000. Each American division, in turn, would have a machine gun battalion as part of its normal table of organization. It was first necessary, of course, to train American soldiers how to use the weapons [6-15]. Once this was achieved, the Yanks took readily to using them. Although most machine guns were employed in a ground support role, later in the war weapons such as the

6-16 American machine gun crew firing at a German airplane.

6-17 American machine gunner, on the second line of defense, firing at a German airplane.

Hotchkiss machine gun would also be used to provide anti-aircraft support [6-16 to 6-18].

Small arms fire, meaning bullets from rifles and machine guns, would account for approximately 39 percent of all battle casualties during the war. An even greater percentage, perhaps as much as 58 percent, would come as a result of artillery and mortar fire. The remainder would come from grenades, bayonets, or other cutting tools such as lances or sabers. Artillery, then, could justly be called the Great War's greatest killer, and those who served in that arm took justifiable pride in their achievements. One such artilleryman was Captain Harry S. Truman, who commanded Battery D of the 129th Field Artillery, 35th Division, a National Guard unit. Truman served in France with distinction, taking good care of his men, showing a high level of military competence, and demonstrating outstanding courage. He was invariably cool under fire, and though like everyone else he often felt fear, he managed to hide it well. He would later say, "The men think I am not much afraid of shells, but they don't know I was too scared to run and that is pretty scared."

Shortages of artillery pieces and shells would plague the American Army throughout the war. In 1917, for example, as the United States was entering the war, the British army had on hand about 76 million shells. The United States, by contrast, had an artillery shell stockpile sufficient for only a nine-hour bombardment [6-19]. As for the artillery pieces themselves, the shortage was equally appalling.

6-18 An old wagon wheel made into a solid revolving base for the Hotchkiss antiaircraft gun.

6-19 A stockpile of artillery shells—note the men regulating the fuses for future use.

In 1917, Pershing and his staff were planning on an AEF force of 500,000 men supported by 2,500 cannon of all calibers. It was a rosy estimate, since that September American foundries would supply only eighty cannon, forty more in October, and none thereafter until June of 1918. By the end of the war, Yank artillerymen would have 2,100 75-mm guns, the vast majority of them purchased from the French, and nearly 1,500 heavy artillery pieces, the latter purchased from both the British and French. They could have used many more, and the lack of sufficient artillery would prove a handicap for the AEF throughout the war.

Famous generals such as Napoléon Bonaparte had long appreciated the use of artillery, and in the American Civil War both Union and Confederate artillery played an important role. Nevertheless, in World War I artillery dominated as never before. Much of this was due to the invention of a breech-loaded weapon with an

6-20 A French 75 loaded with gas shells—note soldiers with gas masks.

effective recoil mechanism, which made it a quick-firing tool of destruction. Undoubtedly the most famous such weapon was the "French 75," kept secret by the French for as long as possible. Its screw-type breech block and recoil mechanism were so superior that other guns came to be modeled after it [6-20]. An almost direct copy was the "German 77" [6-21].

Artillery fired three types of shells: chemical shells for delivering gas or smoke, fragmentation or high explosive shells, and shrapnel. High explosive shells (HE) would split and hurl jagged pieces of steel in all directions. Their fuses might be set to explode on impact, as against troops in the open, or for delayed action if the shells were intended to penetrate an enemy's dugout.

Although "shrapnel" shells were often confused with those of the high explosive variety, they were actually quite different. Whereas an HE shell got its effect by releasing irregular steel fragments, a shrapnel shell, used almost exclusively in an anti-

6-21 American soldiers loading a captured German 77mm gun.

6-22 Entrance to the 16th Infantry Regiment Headquarters blocked by rubble.

6-23 A counterbattery weapon being used as an anti-aircraft gun.

6-24 105mm Howitzers in action.

personnel role, utilized dozens of small lead balls, each the size of a small marble, and with great penetrating capability. Shrapnel shells were set to explode in mid-air as they neared the ground, creating an effect almost like that from a large shotgun.

A common use of artillery, particularly that of a heavier variety, was to prepare the way for an attack by a prolonged bombardment. Although such a bombardment meant the loss of surprise, the results were considered well worthwhile. In response, the front-line infantry could only hunker down in their trenches and dugouts, hoping to avoid a direct hit, and wait for the inevitable assault. The Germans were especially good at this, and were credited with developing the "rolling barrage," which advanced by increments ahead of attacking troops. Attacking ground troops naturally appreciated this, although they also feared that rapidly advancing soldiers might move under their own fire or that short rounds might result in "friendly fire" casualties. Both sides would make frequent use of "rolling" or "creeping" barrages when they launched an attack.

In addition to its antipersonnel role, shellfire might be used against opposing artillery (counterbattery fire), against an enemy headquarters [6-22], to wipe out fortified weapons emplacements, to cut wire, or in an antiaircraft role [6-23].

In addition to their purchased "French 75's," Americans made good use of 105mm and 155mm howitzers [6-24, 6-25]. German artillerymen had weapons of similar caliber, such as the 150 mm, and it was not uncommon for Americans to turn captured German howitzers against their former owners [6-26 to 6-29].

6-25 A Japanese observer (center right) inspecting a 155mm howitzer.

6-26 Men of the 23rd Infantry Regiment use a captured German howitzer against their enemy.

6-27 Another captured German howitzer being used by U.S. soldiers of the 15th Field Artillery.

6-28 Lieutenant Robert Crane, 15th Field Artillery, operates a German 150mm gun.

After the first few weeks of the war, the opposing sides had dug in, and the lines were solidified. Frontal attacks seemed futile, and with the lines solidly established on either end, flanking attacks were impossible. How then, could anyone achieve a breakthrough? As early as December 1914, a creative young British officer, Ernest Swinton, had proposed a bulletproof cross-country vehicle that could bring firepower to the point of assault. One who picked up on the idea was Winston Churchill [6-30]. In a letter to Herbert Asquith, Churchill wrote that "it would be quite easy in a short time to fit up a number of steam tractors with small armored shelters, in which men and machine guns could be placed, which would be bulletproof. Used at night, they would not be affected by artillery fire to any extent. The caterpillar system would enable trenches to be crossed quite easily, and the weight of the machine would destroy all barbed wire

6-29 American soldiers pose by German guns turned over to them on Armistice Day, November 11, 1918.

entanglements." With the enthusiastic support of Churchill and others, the idea was pursued. At the British Admiralty, Churchill began developing what were called, to mislead any enemy spies, "tanks." By December 1915, the Admiralty had developed a tank prototype, "Little Willie." On January 29, 1916, it began its trials. (Optimistically, in July 1918 Churchill would place an order in the United States for 10,000 "cross-country caterpillar vehicles" for delivery in the spring of 1919. However, only

6-30 Winston Churchill (right) with David Lloyd George (left).

6-31 A small British tank put out of action near Chaudon, France.

6-32 An Allied tank emerging from the woods near Breteuil, France.

6-33 An American tank from Company C, 327th Tank Battalion, in action at St. Mihiel, France.

6-34 French tank waiting for the command to go into action near Gutrey, France, on July 16, 1918.

6-35 A French tank near Breteuil, France, on May 11, 1918.

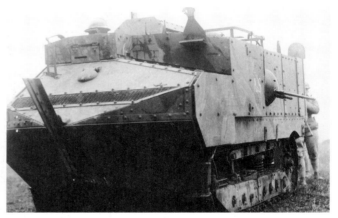

6-36 Another French tank operating near Breteuil.

seventy-nine tanks were manufactured in the United States during the war, and only fifteen ever reached France.)

Eventually the British, French, and Germans would all produce tanks of various shapes and sizes [6-31 to 6-37]. As tactics began to evolve, it became obvious that tanks should be used in massed formations, even though they might also be used individually in support of attacking infantry [6-38]. For many months, however, massed attacks weren't pos-

6-37 A large German tank put out of action during a counter-attack by a direct hit from a 75mm cannon.

6-38 Infantry advancing with support from a tank.

sible, simply because the tanks didn't exist in the necessary numbers.

Not until September 1916 would tanks appear on the battlefield for the first time. On the Somme, forty-nine tanks took part in the attack and were able to advance on a wide front. Ten of the tanks were hit by German artillery fire, nine broke down with mechanical difficulties, and five failed to advance. Nevertheless, those managing to keep going had measurable success, securing a long-sought objective and capturing three villages.

In April 1917, French tanks went into action for the first time in support of the ill-fated offensive launched by General Nivelle. None of the little two-man Renault tanks was able to reach the German front line, almost all bogging down in the scarred, uneven ground. On the whole, tanks of World War I were clumsy, lumbering beasts, and poorly designed. All were subject to frequent breakdowns [6-39], and some, with a vulnerable gas tank placed in front, became little more than mobile Molotov cocktails. Like the air-

plane, the tank accounted for a relatively minor number of casualties, and neither weapon greatly affected the outcome of the war.

In the Great War, as in every war throughout history, transportation to support the fighting troops was all-important. The difference this time was the relatively new internal combustion engine. For the first time in warfare, the truck came into its own [6-40, 6-41]. So did other motorized vehicles, including ambulances and motorcycles [6-42, 6-43]. The noble horse

6-39 An American tank in trouble near Nonsard, France.

6-40 Signal Corps trucks of the 1st Division being loaded with equipment for the front.

6-41 5th Marine Regiment (coming down the road) preparing to leave Sommedieue, France, in trucks. French soldiers are in the foreground.

6-42 Ambulances of the 26th Infantry Division near the front.

6-43 An American motorcycle drawing attention from French medics (at right).

6-44 Horse-drawn caissons in transit near the front.

6-45 18th Infantry Regiment machine gun crew equipment being drawn by horses.

6-46 Horse-driven caissons on their way to the front near the Ardennes, France.

was still very important, although cavalry squadrons were almost a thing of the past. Horses were mostly used for pulling wagons or caissons [6-44 to 6-46] or as mounts for individual officers [6-47]. Toward the end of the war, as vehicles and fuel became increasingly scarce, even that old standby, the bicycle, started appearing with increased frequency [6-48, 6-49].

Throughout the war, American transportation was plagued by

shortages. Ironically, this was the country where Henry Ford's Model T car had first appeared in 1908, with more than a million being produced by 1915. And though it was the nation that had invented cheap, mass-produced, internal combustion engine vehicles, it was never able to provide enough trucks and buses for its own troops.

For the most part, however, supplies and ammunition got through, even though most of it was hauled in vehicles bought from American Allies. The all-important rations also got through. It's true that "an army marches on its stomach," and thanks to Yank perseverance, the World War I Doughboy continued to march.

6-47 Brigadier General B. B. Buck mounted on "Coley," his favorite horse.

6-48 and 6-49 German officers and soldiers turning over their bicycles and equipment to the Americans, November 18, 1918.

SEVEN

Yanks in the Trenches

Yanks in the Trenches

As of October 21, 1917, three American battalions of the 1st Division were on line under the control of the French 18th Division, occupying trenches in a supposedly quiet sector. Everyone appreciated the Americans finally participating, but the Allies wanted to see far more of them, and soon. Still, the French were concerned about the Yanks' combat readiness, and they feared that a setback at this early stage might inhibit U.S. willingness to pour in more troops. Therefore General Paul Emile Bordeaux, the 18th Division commander, a cautious man by nature, became even more so.

Bordeaux, an amiable, friendly man, made it clear he was happy to have the Yanks join him. He was determined, however, not to have anything untoward happen while they were his responsibility. To maintain control, he had each American battalion assigned to a different French regiment. A battalion would man the trenches for ten days to become oriented, then another battalion from the same regiment would take its place. One American artillery battery could fire in support during this time, but only to supplement fires from Bordeaux's own artillery. As an

added precaution, the Doughboys were forbidden to send out patrols beyond their own barbed wire. This left Germans controlling the night, free to roam about No Man's Land while Americans hunkered down in soggy, rat-infested trenches, became tense, and endured the intermittent shelling. All in all, however, things were proceeding on schedule, and the first Doughboy units seemed to be adapting to trench warfare [7-1]. It became rather routine, even when the first Yank was wounded on October 24 and treated at an American field hospital at Einville [7-2], or

7-1 Doughboys in the trenches, Einville, Meurthe et Moselle, France, March 1918.

7-2 Wounded soldier of the 16th Infantry Regiment.

when on October 27 a German prisoner was captured by members of the U.S. 18th Infantry Regiment.

Elsewhere, things were going badly for the Allies that fall. In Italy on October 24 a combined Austrian and German offensive at Caporetto broke through on a broad front. The Germans inflicted 40,000 casualties, captured 300,000 prisoners, and seized 3,000 artillery pieces. To the east, the Russian army was barely a factor. Revolution had broken out the previous March, and Czar Nicholas had been forced to abdicate in favor of a provisional government, one that would last but a few months. People in the States seemed to approve. A photo in the *New York Times* was captioned, "The New Born Freedom of Russia's Armies." The accompanying article said, "It is now as much a matter of course for the soldiers to hold meetings and discussions as for the civilians of the most

democratic countries. . . . And so, thoroughly imbued as the Russian revolutionaries are with the doctrines of international socialism, a great new offensive has been launched." It didn't take long for things to change. By November the Bolsheviks had taken over, and Vladimir Lenin, the newly elected Chairman of the People's Commissars, had seized power. On November 8 he called for an end to hostilities, in effect telling the Russian soldiers to lay down their arms.

Back in the sector of the French 18th Division, the routine would soon be shattered. The Germans had learned about Americans coming on line and decided to give them a proper "reception." Bavarian shock troops (one Yank called them "the widely-advertised cutthroats of the German army") were chosen to initiate Americans to combat and perhaps make them fearful of things to come. On the night of November 2–3, the 2nd

Battalion of the 16th Infantry Regiment had just relieved the regiment's 1st Battalion, and after the normal confusion, things were settling down. About 3 A.M., after an initial shelling, the Germans shifted to a "box barrage," isolating a single platoon of Company F. Shellfire erupted on each of the platoon's flanks and to its rear, cutting off any chance of reinforcements. Then the raiding party swooped down. It was soon over. After fifteen minutes the Bavarians returned to their own lines, carrying with them eleven prisoners and leaving behind three American dead: Corporal James R. Gresham and Privates Merle D. Hay and Thomas F. Enright [7-3 to 7-5]. When Enright's body was found, it appeared that he had been captured but had refused to accompany his captors. He must have fought hard, for in retaliation the enemy had cut his throat and ripped open his chest. A medical officer later counted

7-3 Corporal James R. Gresham.

7-4 Private Merle D. Hay.

7-5 Private Thomas F. Enright.

7-6 The graves of the first three American soldiers to die in France.

Great Republic of the United States who died on the soil of France for Justice and Liberty." The *New York Tribune* summed it up well: "Our playing at war is over."

Soon after the incident, Major Theodore Roosevelt, Jr., son of the former president, asked permission to make a retaliatory raid [7-8]. General Bordeaux, who considered the raid of November 3 but a minor affair,

twelve bayonet wounds on Enright's body. The *New York Times*, reporting on "OUR BOYS' FIRST BRUSH WITH THE ENEMY," said the Yanks "fought gallantly until overwhelmed solely by numbers. . . . Pistols, grenades, knives, and bayonets were used freely during the short and extremely fierce hand-to-hand encounter."

The next day, the three Americans were buried with honors at Bathelemont, a small town just behind the lines where they had fallen. General Bordeaux himself conducted the service, saying, "The death of his humble Corporal and these Privates appeals to us with unwonted

grandeur. We will, therefore, ask that the mortal remains of the young men be left with us forever. We will inscribe on their tombs, 'here lie the first soldiers of the United States to fall on the fields of France for justice' . . . . Corporal Gresham, Private Enright, and Private Hay, in the name of France I thank you. God receive your souls" [7-6].

Pershing visited the graves, saluted, and stood bareheaded for a moment [7-7]. The French government gave each man a Croix de Guerre and later erected a small monument in their honor. On it was engraved: "Here lie the First Soldiers of the

7-8 Major Theodore Roosevelt, Jr.

7-7 The funeral service for Gresham, Enright, and Hay attended by American and French officers.

at first refused his permission. The enthusiastic Roosevelt persisted, and out of respect for his famous father, permission was finally granted, both from Bordeaux and from General Sibert. The detachment making the raid was a unit commanded by Theodore's younger brother, Archie. Two sons of a former president going on the same raid—a raid that would normally be led by a sergeant! That was too much. Theodore, Jr., was forced to stay behind. The raid itself, led by Archie, came off without incident and without enemy contact. In the confusing darkness, the only "action" turned out to be an exchange of fire with friendly French troops. Fortunately no one was hurt.

The debacle at Caporetto had emphasized the need for greater cooperation and coordination between Allies. As a result, a Supreme War Council was established on November 7 following a conference at Rapallo, Italy. The Council's permanent home was set up at Versailles, and the Council's announced mission was to take charge of the overall conduct of the war. Although Pershing liked the idea in principle, he thought an even better idea would be to appoint a Supreme Allied Commander. This was unlikely, however, for in Pershing's opinion, "the French would object to any but a Frenchman, and the English might not like that." Pershing also knew that both Haig and Petain opposed the idea. As a result, Pershing, when invited to attend the Council conference, had respectfully declined, not wanting to be caught in the middle. Also, he didn't think it right to attend without specifically being asked to do so by his government.

The political members of the Council were the three Allied heads of state: David Lloyd George of England, Paul Painleve of France, and Vittorio Orlando of Italy. President Wilson did not participate, nor did he send a diplomatic representative, since at this stage he considered the U.S. an "associate" rather than an ally. He did however, send his trusted adviser, "Colonel" Edward House, to attend [7-9]. Military men on the Council were Marshal Foch for France, General Wilson for Britain, and General Cadorna for Italy. The military representative for the U.S. was the U.S. Army chief-of-staff, Major General Tasker H. Bliss [7-10]. Bliss, nominated by Secretary of War Newton Baker for the job, was an excellent choice. Although Baker said Bliss "probably could not have drilled a squad," he had other skills, notably the tact and diplomacy that Pershing lacked. In addition, as a scholar and a linguist, he fitted in well with the diplomats on the Council. One observer said Bliss had such tremendous learning that he would have been an ornament to university faculty, provided his fellow professors could get used to feeling second-rate in his presence. Baker later said that Bliss "had in a higher degree than anybody else with whom I have ever been in contact the habit of deliberate and consecutive thinking . . . [his] mind was a comprehensive card index." In short, while Bliss could not have done Pershing's job, Pershing could not have done his.

7-9 Colonel Edward House, President Wilson's adviser.

7-10 Major General Tasker H. Bliss.

Soon there was general public grumbling about the War Council in both France and England, where people saw it as an encroachment on national sovereignty. In France, when Painleve was pushed out of office and replaced by Georges Clemenceau at the end of November, public disaffection with the Council was probably a factor.

For several weeks, Pershing had been concerned about the leadership of the 1st Division. These men were Pershing's "show horses," presumably the best the regular army could put in the field. Yet when he inspected them, he found them to be sloppy and undisciplined. In September President Poincare of France, along with several other dignitaries, had accompanied Pershing to watch a 1st Division review [7-11]. It had gone badly, with troops marching out of step while looking both ragged and unkempt. Actually much of this could have been excused. The request for a review had been issued on the spur of the

moment, and had been received at 1st Division headquarters only the preceding evening. Some of the troops had come from widely scattered locations and had to march most of the night to be on hand. Pershing wasn't listening to any excuses. He made no secret of his annoyance and became increasingly displeased with the 1st Division's commander, the easygoing Sibert.

A month later, Pershing visited the 1st Division again, this time to watch a demonstration of a battalion attack on a fortified position. The demonstration went well. Sibert, however, when asked to critique the attack, seemed unfamiliar with the scenario. Shortly thereafter Sibert was informed that he was being relieved. (He returned to the States, where he became Director of the Chemical Warfare Service.)

Pershing's evaluation of Sibert was brutal: "slow of speech and of thought. . . . Slovenly in dress. . . . Without any ability as a soldier. . . . Utterly hopeless as an instructor or tactician, fails to

appreciate soldierly qualities, possessing none himself. . . . Opinionated withal and difficult to teach. He had a very high opinion of his own worth."

To replace Sibert, Pershing named fifty-six-year-old Robert Lee Bullard, West Point class of 1885, a no-nonsense officer with a reputation for toughness. Bullard, in fact, once told someone he considered Pershing "soft." In any case, Bullard made clear what he expected from his officers and men as he wrote, "I took over here on December 14th and General Sibert departed for the States. Since that day I've been going at a high rate of speed. Everyone and everything is working under heavy pressure. I think I've scared 'em all by telling them that they'd be 'relieved' without any hesitation if they did not 'deliver the goods'; they must succeed or would lose their commands [7-12].

Arriving in France that December was the 369th Infantry Regiment, a nearly

7-11 General Pershing (left) and President Raymond Poincare (second from left) with other officer and dignitaries observing troops.

7-12 General Pershing (second from right) and General Bullard (right) and their staffs in Tartigny, France, June 1918.

all-black National Guard unit. Supposedly this was a combat outfit, but it was never trained for combat nor ever given a chance to fight. Under the racist climate that prevailed during World War I (and much of World War II), blacks were mainly assigned to perform manual labor in service units, given tasks such as stevedores unloading cargo or helping engineers to dig ditches [7-13]. No black Americans were permitted to serve alongside whites in a combat unit, and in regiments

7-13 Soldiers of Company B, 4th Engineer, 2nd Division, preparing a bombing trench, Nanteuil-sur-Marne, France, June 1918.

such as the 369th that managed to get to France (and that after a hard struggle), the officers were nearly all white. Racism in America was a fact of life, and bigotry ran just as deep or deeper throughout the AEF.

By the end of 1917, the U.S. had four infantry divisions in France. Two of these were regular army units assembled in France: the "Big Red One" 1st Division at Gondrecourt, now led by Bullard, and the 2nd Division at Bourmont, commanded by Omar Bundy [7-14]. The 2nd contained not only Army units but also a brigade of Marines, complete with band [7-15]. In addition, there were two National Guard

7-14 Major General Omar Bundy.

7-15 U.S. Marine band.

7-17 A joint French-American training exercise near Gondrecourt, France, October 1917. The French soldiers are in the foreground.

7-16 Major General Hunter Liggett.

divisions: the 42nd (Rainbow) Division commanded by Charles Menoher, stationed at Bourmont, about halfway between Neufchateau and Chaumont, and Clarence Edwards's 26th (Yankee) Division, also at Bourmont. Pershing, it might be noted, was skeptical about Edwards, who although a West Pointer from the class of 1883 tended to act superior to the regular army because of the elite nature of his organization with its collection of New England bluebloods. He also was given to exaggerating the hardships his men were undergoing and to complaining about higher headquarters. So far, however, Edwards had done nothing

glaringly wrong, and Pershing kept him on.

In January 1918, Pershing combined his four divisions into what he designated the First American Army Corps, with headquarters at Neufchateau. He named Major General Hunter Liggett as corps commander [7-16]. This was in keeping with Pershing's long-held goal of combining an American force and putting it on line in its own sector *and* under American control.

Shortly before, Bullard had been told to take his 1st Division on line, where it would be under the control of a French corps commander, General Eugene Debeney. Bullard had no illusions as to what was expected. He knew his men had trained hard to learn individual soldier skills, had even practiced fire and movement in attacks of regimental scale [7-17]. That was in keeping with General Pershing's

philosophy. "We're not going to win this war by slugging it out in the trenches," Pershing said. "At some point we must break through the Hindenburg Line, and when we do, I want us to know what to do when we get out in the open."

Now it was time for the Doughboys to prove themselves. Bullard told his staff, "Pershing is looking for results. He intends to have them. He will sacrifice any man who does not bring them." In mid-January 1918, the 1st Division moved into territory that was part of the St. Mihiel salient, taking over from the French 1st Moroccan Division. The whole division was operating as a unit for the first time.

Bit by bit, that winter of 1917–18, Americans were entering the line and encountering the ugliness of war. They went forward over roads that were in-

7-18 Company B, 26th Infantry Regiment, 1st Division, on their way to the front near Royaumeix, France, March 1918.

7-19 1st Trench Mortar Battery, 1st Division, on their way to the front, January 1918.

variably muddy and often icy [7-18, 7-19]. They also encountered especially bitter weather, with one of the coldest French winters in years [7-20]. Winter clothing, requisitioned back in

July, had failed to arrive in sufficient quantities. For both the military and civilians, coal shortages also became a problem, and it was learned that French mines were operating well below

7-20 Barracks of the 1st Engineers in the cold and snow, Gondrecourt, France, January 1918.

capacity because of a shortage of manpower. Charles Dawes said he might be able to help, offering to examine the possibility of bringing over experienced American coal miners. The French, however, declined the offer. Importing American miners, they said, would cause a serious problem with French trade unions.

When Yank units arrived to occupy trenches formerly held by the Moroccans, they found themselves looking at a twisted tangle of barbed wire to their front and, perhaps two hundred yards farther away, similar wire belonging to the enemy. The trench itself was filled with mud, assorted debris, and a repulsive stench, much of which came from an accumulation of decaying, unburied bodies in No Man's Land. There was usually an underground shelter where officers worked by candlelight amid what one called "sewer-like odors." A typical day began with a "stand-to" at dawn, the most likely time for an enemy attack. Sometimes this was followed by a "morning hate," when both sides poured forth a volume of fire. After breakfast, fatigue duties were performed, and those off-duty tried to catch some sleep. At dusk the "stand-to" and "hate" session were repeated [7-21 to 7-24]. Hot food was generally served after dark, having been prepared in the rear and brought forward by carrying parties [7-25].

On February 5, the United States suffered a severe loss at

7-21 1st Infantry Division in front line trenches, Ansauville sector.

7-22 1st Infantry Division soldiers on guard duty in a lookout trench.

7-23 A dugout used by the 1st Division as a shelter from artillery bombardment.

7-24 American 1st Division troops in the front line trenches, early 1918.

7-25 Field kitchen of the 1st Division near Meurthe-et-Moselle, France, November 1917.

7-26 Smoke screen used by an 18th Infantry Regiment raiding party, Gondrecourt, France, October 1917.

7-27 Paul Meier (center), 259th German Reserve, taken prisoner by U.S. 18th Infantry in a raid, Menil-la-tour, France, March 1918.

sea when the troopship *Tuscania* was sunk by a German submarine, with 113 men losing their lives. The *Tuscania* was a Cunard-owned liner, a sister ship to the better known *Lusitania*. When she put to sea, at 550 feet and 14,348 tons gross, she was considered the prize of the Anchor Line's fleet before being turned over to Cunard for use as a troop ship. She stayed afloat for several hours after being hit,

giving men enough time to launch lifeboats. The weather was foul, however, and the sea was turbulent. Some of the boats crashed against rocks on the Irish coast, sweeping men into black, icy waters, where they quickly drowned.

On February 5, the day of the *Tuscania* sinking, General Bullard issued an order to men of the 1st Division, making it clear he did not intend to wait

passively for the war to come to him. His instructions began:

1. There are no orders which require us to wait for the enemy to fire on us before we fire on him; do not wait

7-28 German prisoners being brought in by 16th Infantry, September 1918.

7-29 More captured Germans being led by American guards.

7-30 German liquid fire machines (flame throwers) captured by men of the 18th Infantry, March 1918.

7-31 A wounded man from the 2nd Division arriving at the 15th Field Hospital near Montreuial, France, June 1918.

7-32 Wounded arriving at the 15th Field Hospital, Montreuial, France, June 1918.

for him to fire first. Be active all over no-man's-land; do not leave its control to the enemy.

2. Front line commanders will immediately locate and report all places where there is a favorable opportunity for strong ambuscades and for raids on the enemy's lines and advance posts.

Raids required special skills, ones that other armies had learned the hard way and paid for in blood. Fortunately the Moroccans had learned these skills and were happy to coach the Americans on raiding techniques, including the use of smoke to provide a screen for raiding parties [7-26]. Bullard's men conducted several such raids, often bringing in prisoners [7-27 to 7-29], or pieces of enemy equipment [7-30]. Close combat of course meant casualties [7-31 to 7-33].

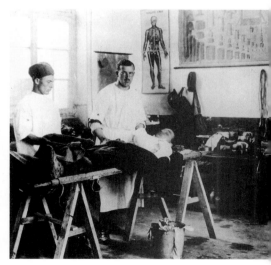

7-33 Private John A. Coolidge of the 1st Field Battalion, Signal Corps, being operated on at the 1st Field Hospital Unit, Bezu, France, June 1918.

7-34 Troops lined up to get food.

7-35 Troops enjoying a meal outside the trenches.

7-36 An unidentified GI enjoys a back scrubbing.

By the time the 1st Division was relieved on March 21, it had suffered 143 killed, 403 wounded, and 3 missing.

It had been a rough few weeks, but the men of the 1st Division were feeling good about themselves. They were proud to have proven themselves in combat, happy to have become blooded veterans, happy to eat hot food in calm surroundings [7-34, 7-35], happy to get cleaned up [7-36, 7-37], happy just to relax [7-38, 7-39].

Back in Washington, Secretary of War Baker decided it was time to reorganize the general staff. With former chief-of-staff Tasker Bliss now assigned as a permanent member of the War Council, a new chief was needed. To fill the slot, Baker selected the highly respected fifty-two-year-old Peyton March [7-40]. March's specialty was artillery. He had come to France as artillery commander of the 1st Division, and in that role he had performed with his usual efficiency, but with a style that was ruthless and abrasive. Although some saw him as a hatchet man, his superior officers considered him a trouble shooter. In any case, Secretary Baker wanted him back in Washington as Army chief-of-staff. March was reluctant to accept the position; like most regular officers he wanted to be close to the action. Pershing also wanted him to remain in France, but then a message from Baker told Pershing to release him, for he was "urgently needed" in Washington. He returned to the States on March 2 and as the new chief-of-staff received his fourth star. This changed things for Pershing, who heretofore had been dealing directly with Secretary Baker and President Wilson. Now he would have to go through March. Those who knew both men suspected there would be friction. They were right.

7-37 GI's washing their clothes.

7-38 Soldiers of the 1st Infantry Division eating dinner immediately behind the first line trenches, near Petit Froissey, France, May 1918.

7-39 Soldiers of the 16th Infantry Regiment entertaining themselves with a piano.

7-40 General Peyton March.

EIGHT

The Home Front

The Home Front

Well before the first Yanks entered combat, people at home were supporting the war enthusiastically. Much of the credit for this belonged to the Committee on Public Information established by Executive Order on April 11, 1917. Heading the Committee was an aggressive, eager-beaver publicity man, George Creel [8-1], who flooded the country with war bulletins on a daily (sometimes hourly) basis. Theoretically, Creel's mission was to oversee the release of government news. Interpreting this broadly, he created a daily newspaper, the "Official Bulletin," under former *Washington Post* editor Edward Sudler, and soon Creel was not only releasing news, he was creating and controlling it.

In the following weeks, Creel enlisted the help of artists, cartoonists, and entertainers to help "sell the war." Slogans appeared such as "making the world safe for democracy" and "the war to end all wars." Artists were urged to "draw 'til it hurts." In response they created some 700 poster designs, 122 streetcar advertising cards, 310 advertising illustrations, and 287 cartoons. The most famous poster to emerge, perhaps the most famous poster of all time, was James Montgomery Flagg's "Uncle Sam Wants

8-1 George Creel.

YOU!" [8-2]. From every angle, Uncle Sam appeared to be looking directly at the viewer and demanding a response.

Information turned into outright propaganda, with Germans described as "barbaric huns" who performed unspeakable atrocities [8-3]. One story claimed that German soldiers often cut off the hands of Belgian schoolboys. (Despite an intensive search, no such victim was ever found.) Nevertheless,

8-2 The famous Uncle Sam recruiting poster.

8-3 Poster urging citizens to buy war bonds.

anti-German sentiment swept the country. Sauerkraut became "liberty noodle strings." Owners of German shepherds began calling them "police dogs." Hamburgers became "Salisbury steak," Wiener Schnitzel was banned from restaurant menus, and some people with German names Anglicized them to avoid discrimination.

There were four Liberty Loan Campaigns, organized by Treasury Secretary William McAdoo, President Wilson's son-in-law. Enthusiastic slogans emerged in support of the Liberty Loan Campaigns, including "Buy Bonds Till It Hurts," "Come Across or the Kaiser Will," "The Soldier Gives—You Must Lend," and "A Bond Slacker Is a Kaiser Backer" [8-4]. Supporting these campaigns, bond rallies were held throughout the country, with appearances by movie stars such as Theda Bara, Douglas Fairbanks, and Mary Pickford. One successful rally was staged on the steps of the New York Public Library, with top entertainers performing. Among these was musical comedy star Elsie Janis [8-5], who had performed for troops in France, where she acquired the nickname "Sweetheart of the AEF." Not long before, her English actor fiancé had been killed in action on the Western Front.

In addition to the bond drives,

8-4 A war bond postcard that urges Americans to buy war bonds but also demonizes the Germans.

there were also collections taken up for agencies such as the Salvation Army [8-6] or to send personal items such as Bibles to individual soldiers overseas [8-7].

Tin Pan Alley, not to be outdone, responded vigorously. George M. Cohan's "Over There" remained the war's most popular song, and the great tenor Enrico Caruso's recording

8-5 Entertainer Elsie Janis, who performed for troops in France.

8-6 Salvation Army canteen in France, June 1918.

8-7 A trench mirror, which along with a New Testament saved a man's life by stopping a bullet, being held by correspondent Bert Ford, Bonvillers, France, May 1918.

of it became the war's best-selling phonograph record. At Camp Upton, near Yaphank, Long Island, Private Irving Berlin wrote music for the soldier show, "Yip, Yip, Yaphank," including the popular "Oh, How I Hate to Get Up in the Morning." Other songs, such as "Good-bye Broadway, Hello France," also written by Berlin, contained lyrics that were supremely patriotic if not always accurate:

> Good-bye, Broadway, hello France,
> We're ten million strong.
> Good-bye sweethearts, wives and mothers,
> It won't take us long.
> Don't you worry while we're gone,
> It's you we're fighting for.
> So good-bye Broadway, hello France,
> WE'RE GONNA' HELP YOU WIN THIS WAR!

Americans of all ages were singing, often to a tune played on the family victrola. General Leonard Wood even said, "It is just as essential that a soldier knows how to sing as that he carry a rifle and shoot it." Overseas, Doughboys sang lustily about the "Mademoiselle from Armentieres" with a few unprintable verses that would never be heard in church. Along these lines, a photo appeared in the newspapers of soldiers advancing to the front while a chaplain gave his blessing. It was captioned, "Onward Christian Soldiers." "As I recall," said one veteran, "at the time we were actually singing 'Bangin' Away on Lulu!'"

The country was turning to wartime production, but slowly. For example, the AEF fired about nine million shells during the war, but only 208,000 of these were American made [8-8]. Even when production was on schedule, there was often a slowdown in getting things to France, both because of shipping shortages and problems with the railroads. Railroads failed to cooperate with each other in transporting war materiel. Thousands of loaded railcars sat idle, and the president of the Pennsylvania Railroad confessed that "The conditions of the railroads presents a menace to the country." The Senate Military Affairs Committee launched an investigation and was outraged by

8-8 Empty artillery shells ready to be loaded.

8-9 Workers removing hot steel from the furnace before sending it to the rolling machine.

8-10 A view showing the length and diameter of hot, rolling steel.

8-11 Hammering steel bars used for gun shields.

what it found. As a consequence, in December of 1917 a presidential proclamation gave the government control of the railroads. Treasury Secretary McAdoo became, in addition to his other duties, czar of the rails.

When General March declared that an army fights and moves on steel, the country responded. Steel mills rearranged priorities, stepped up their production [8-9 to 8-11], and the resulting steel became the needed raw material for arms manufacture [8-12, 8-13]. Simultaneously, civilian uses of steel were drastically reduced, and scrap drives were held. New York City ripped out 5,000 of its 35,000 lampposts and shipped them to arsenals where they could be melted down. Women helped by casting aside traditional corsets and donating their metal stays to the cause, enough, one wag suggested, to make two battleships!

Shipbuilding remained a high

8-12 A factory producing guns for the U.S. military.

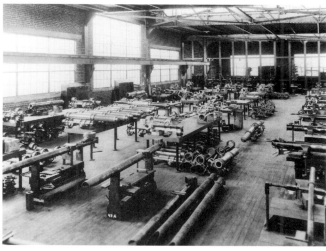

8-13 Limbers and caissons being manufactured at the Bethlehem Steel Co. in Bethlehem, Pennsylvania.

8-14 A merchant ship in its final stage of building.

priority, with working hours being expanded and shipyards hiring thousands of new workers [8-14 to 8-18]. It was a constant struggle to keep up with the expanding need for getting more war materiel to France despite the constant U-boat sinkings. Also, sabotage, at shipyards and factories, had been taking place even before America entered the war, with eighty-eight suspicious accidents and acts of proven sabotage occurring between the beginning of 1915 and January of 1917 alone. On July 30, 1916, one of the most notorious incidents transpired at the Lehigh Valley Railroad's Black Tom terminal on the New Jersey side of the Hudson River, where enemy agents had placed incendiary bombs on several munitions barges. Although only three were killed in the resulting blasts, the explosions wrecked the terminal, destroyed millions of dollars in munitions, and blew out windows all across lower Manhattan. Tales of real or suspected sabotage, allegedly the work of German spies, continued to be of concern throughout the war, with security being provided by

8-15 Lowering the stern of the ship into place.

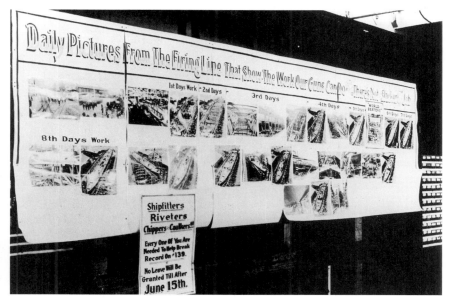

8-16 A progress photo posted on a bulletin board of a ship being built at an unknown shipyard.

8-17 Certificate of enrollment for U.S. shipyard volunteers.

8-18 Shipyard workers attending a patriotic meeting during their lunch hour.

8-19 Sentry duty at an east coast shipyard.

8-20 Female workers at a rubber factory in Ohio.

8-21 Vocational training for women at a machine shop of the Packard Motor Company in Detroit, Michigan.

armed guards at critical installations [8-19].

Meanwhile a cultural change was taking place, as large numbers of women were entering the workforce [8-20]. They were employed in a variety of occupations, with training programs set up to prepare them for jobs previously reserved for men. The YWCA held many such schools, as did various industries. One such school was held at the machine shop of the Packard

8-22 Women workers in Yonkers, New York, at the Habershaw Wire & Cable Corporation.

8-23 Women working at a clothing factory.

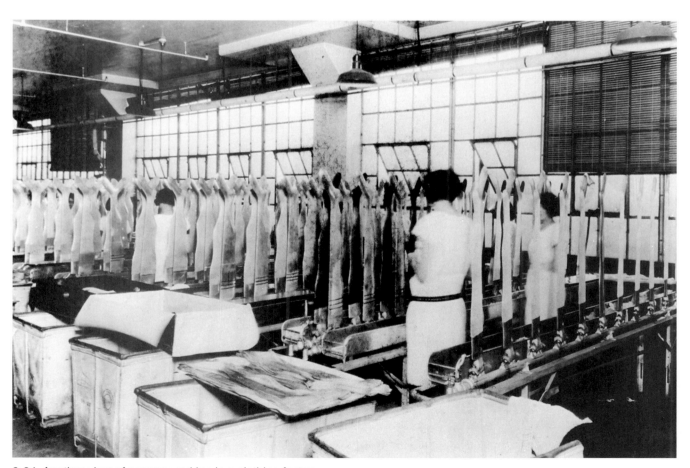

8-24 Another view of women working in a clothing factory.

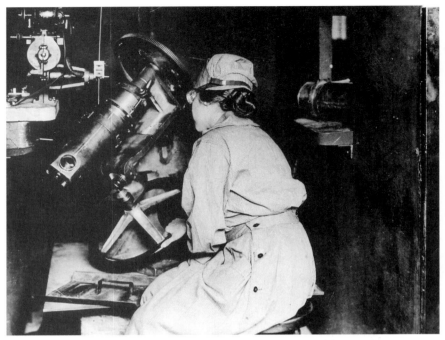

8-25 A woman welding a cylinder of a Liberty ship engine at the Nordyke and Marmon Company, a plant in Indianapolis, Indiana.

8-26 Women airplane builders.

Motor Company [8-21]. Women began delivering Western Union telegrams, serving as elevator operators, working in munitions factories [8-22], and making clothing [8-23, 8-24]. Some even learned to be welders [8-25]. Many women were also working in the newly expanded aircraft factories [8-26, 8-27], though as it turned out, practically no plane manufactured in America ever made it to France during World War I. Altogether, the home front in World War I, with its music, war bond drives, and factory and shipyard workers of both sexes, became the model for the next big war, World War II.

8-27 Three women with the first wing panel made in a manufacturing department, Naval Aircraft Factory, Philadelphia Navy Yard.

NINE

The Crucial Months:

March–July 1918

The Crucial Months:
March–July 1918

In March 1918, Secretary of War Newton Baker arrived in France to see the AEF firsthand [9-1]. The diminutive secretary mostly wanted to visit the front, where by this time Americans were beginning to see action. Pershing, however, acting as Baker's escort, decided first to show him what was happening in the rear areas. The War Department, Pershing said, could best help the AEF by emphasizing the needs of the rapidly growing Services of Supply and the lines of communication. Baker and Pershing inspected the busy port facilities at St. Nazaire [9-2], after which they visited a base hospital at Savenay, where Pershing was pleased by the military appearance of the nurses [9-3]. At Tours, the Services of Supply headquarters, Baker met with the commander, General Francis Kernan. Later, at Issoudon, the main Air Service School, the secretary was impressed by the sight of hundreds of Yanks engaged in pilot training. Then Baker and Pershing were off to the 1st Divi-

9-1 Secretary of War Newton D. Baker leaving 1st Division headquarters.

9-2 The port at St. Nazaire, France.

9-3 Nurse with Secretary Baker (left) and General Pershing (center) at St. Savenay Hospital.

9-4 The 16th Infantry Regiment passing in review.

sion area, where the division's 16th Infantry Regiment held a review in their honor [9-4]. The "Big Red One" had remained aggressive, conducting frequent raids, and days earlier some of its members had been decorated for heroism [9-5]. Baker next visited the 42nd Rainbow Division, where he crawled through a communications trench to visit the front then insisted on going still further to an observation post only a few yards from the enemy. Throughout the trip, Baker, a former Cleveland mayor and ever a politician, made it a point to visit with soldiers from Ohio [9-6]. It was a whirlwind tour, but Baker liked what he saw. The visit, he told the press, had brought him "a great uplift in spirit." He may not have realized that his visit had been conducted during a lull before the storm.

German General Erich von Ludendorff was a fine strategist. He was also a realist. Although the flow of Americans troops was being slowed by the U-boat campaign, Ludendorff recognized that inevitably there would be millions of young Americans joining the Allied armies. Once that happened, Germany's fate would be sealed. His best chance, Ludendorff decided, was to launch an all-out "win the war"

9-5 Members of the the "Big Red One" Infantry Division being decorated for heroism.

9-6 Secretary Baker (left) poses with Private Carlisle Babcock of Headquarters 2nd Division in March 1918.

offensive before all those Yanks arrived on the scene.

The treaty of Brest-Litovsk between Germany and Russia was signed on March 3, 1918, which meant Germany's troops in Russia could now be moved to the Western Front. With additional forces available to him, Ludendorff launched his major Somme offensive on March 21. Following a massive

9-7 Ferdinand Foch, Supreme Allied Commander.

artillery barrage, thirty-two German divisions smashed into the British 5th Army. Twenty-eight supporting divisions followed, attacking under the cover of still more artillery and poison gas. The British front collapsed into chaotic confusion, and Ludendorff had his breakthrough. It was a situation calling for better Allied co-ordination, and on March 26, the War Council named Ferdinand Foch [9-7] to become the Supreme Allied Commander.

For months Pershing had been arguing that green Doughboy divisions should not be committed prematurely into combat. At the same time, he had continued to press for an American Army acting independently in its own sector. In response, the Supreme War Council met, with Pershing in attendance, and agreed that "an American Army should be formed as early as possible under its own commander under its own flag." That was the theory, but the present crisis made that impossible.

On March 28 Pershing drove nearly all day over muddy, congested roads to Foch's headquarters at Clermont-sur-Oise. Arriving late in the evening, he found Foch bent over a map spread on a kitchen table. "I have come," Pershing said, "to tell you that the American people would consider it a great honor for our troops to be engaged in the present battle. I ask you for this in their name and my own."

It was an emotional moment. Foch, gripping Pershing's arms, thanked him profusely. Both men knew, however, that the American's gesture was mostly symbolic. Of the six U.S. divisions in France, only the "Big Red One" had had combat experience. Nevertheless, the raw new divisions were sent into quiet sectors along the line, freeing ten French divisions for the relief of the British. By this time, fortunately, the German offensive had largely run its course, giving everyone some temporary breathing room.

On April 4 Clarence Edwards's 26th "Yankee" Division replaced Bullard's 1st Division on line. The relief did not go smoothly as, despite Bullard's best efforts, the self-important Edwards filed a series of complaints about everything he saw. Pershing, no fan of Edwards, told Bullard not to worry about it. Bullard's men, for their part, were just happy to get out of the trenches, to rest, and to get cleaned up [9-8, 9-9].

Elsewhere the situation was desperate, and on April 11 General Douglas Haig issued what became known as his "back to the wall" order: "There is no other course open to us but to fight it out. Every position must be held to the last man. There must be no retirement. With our backs to the wall and believing in the justice of our cause each one must fight on to the end. The safety of our home and the freedom of mankind alike depend upon the conduct of

9-8 Machine Gun Company, 18th Infantry Regiment, 1st Division, on their first day out of the trenches.

9-9 An American infantryman cleaning mud from his *puttees* [cloth leggings].

each one of us at this critical moment."

On 20 April, near the village of Seicheprey, the 26th (Yankee) Division saw its first serious fighting. Following a heavy artillery bombardment, about 3,000 special storm troops (known as Hindenburg's Traveling Circus) advanced through a heavy fog and caught the Americans by surprise. In what was intended only as a raid, the Germans inflicted 669 casualties, with 81 dead, 187 wounded, 214 gassed, and 187 captured or reported missing. Pershing was furious, not just because of the casualties, but because the division's poor performance reflected so badly on the American Army. In Pershing's mind, it was another strike against Edwards, the division commander. Edwards had powerful political supporters in Congress, so for the moment Pershing felt unable to fire him. Edwards therefore retained command of the division and saw it through the heavy fighting that lay ahead. Six months later, however, by which time Pershing was in a much stronger personal position, Edwards would be sacked.

Casualties tested the newly established hospital system, and it performed well. Some men were treated at front-line aid stations [9-10]. More severely wounded went to a regional hospital [9-11], or to a hospital ship for a return to England or America [9-12].

The debacle at Seicheprey had been a major embarrassment, and the American Army needed to restore its reputation, preferably through an all-American operation. By the end of May the AEF had eleven combat divisions in France and England. Six of these were committed. The 1st

9-10 1st Division, First Aid Station—note how it is concealed from observation by trees and camouflage.

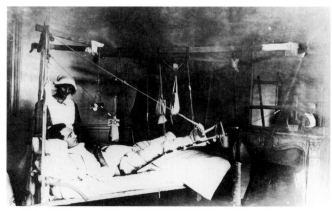

9-11 Corporal Nick Treger, Company D, 16th Infantry, being attended to at Red Cross Hospital No. 2 in Paris.

9-12 Wounded on stretchers being placed aboard the hospital ship *Mercy* at St. Nazaire for transportation to America.

9-13 General Pershing addressing the officers of the 16th and 18th Infantries at Gondrecourt, France, March 1918.

9-14 A battery of the 5th Field Artillery, 1st Division, on the road near Toul, France, where they will board a train for the British-French front, March 1918.

9-15 The 6th Field Artillery, 1st Division, placing guns in position at Missy-aux-Bois, France, July 1918.

Division was with the French near Amiens; the 2nd, 26th, and 42nd, were in quiet sectors nearby, while the 32nd and 77th were about to go on line.

The village of Cantigny was chosen as the objective of an assault that would demonstrate American capability. Pershing gave the task to his trusted 1st Division. Speaking directly to the officers and men who would make the attack [9-13], he urged them to "wipe out the stain of Seicheprey." For once

dropping his characteristic reserve, he spoke to them in emotional terms: "You are going to meet a savage enemy, flushed with victory. Meet him like Americans. When you hit, hit hard, and don't stop hitting. You don't know the meaning of the word defeat!"

The attack was well planned and well executed. A mock battlefield was laid out behind the lines where troops practiced the assault. As they made their plans, key officers and noncoms

studied large sand tables that simulated the terrain. Aerial photographs were taken, and artillery was moved into position [9-14, 9-15]. Men waited nervously in trenches [9-16], and on May 28, after a two-hour artillery barrage beginning at 4:45 A.M., the signal was given to go "over the top." Supported by French tanks, machine gun fire [9-17], and a rolling artillery barrage, lines of Doughboys moved forward under cover of smoke.

9-16 Members of the 132nd Infantry, Illinois National Guard, in the front line trenches expecting an attack any moment, near the Meuse River, France, September 1918.

9-17 A gun crew from Regimental Headquarters Company, 23rd Infantry Regiment, 2nd Division, firing a 37mm gun during an advance against German entrenched positions.

By 7:30 A.M. Cantigny was taken [9-18], but the worst was yet to come. Many of the town's German defenders had taken cover during the artillery barrage. Now they emerged from cellars and foxholes to engage the Americans, often in hand-to-hand fighting. Then, following a huge artillery bombardment, a wave of German infantry counterattacked the village. At one point Major Theodore Roosevelt, Jr., son of the former president, led a battalion of the 26th Infantry across the fields in front of Cantigny to plug a gap [9-19]. Over the next two days, other violent counterattacks were repulsed, and finally the German defenders of Cantigny had either been killed or captured. Hundreds of prisoners were marched to the rear and placed under guard for further interrogation [9-20, 9-21].

Cantigny was a definite success and did wonders for morale and to restore American prestige. But it did not come without a price:

the 1st Division's total losses and evacuations came to some 1,300 men. Division Commander Bullard, while admitting Cantigny was a small fight in the overall scheme of things, would say, "Hundreds [of fights] greater had preceded and would follow it in the mighty war. But Cantigny was, nevertheless, one of the most important engagements of the war in its import to our war-

wearied and sorely tried Allies. To both friend and foe it said, 'Americans will both fight and stick.'"

On May 28, the very day of the Cantigny attack, Brigadier General Dennis Nolan, Pershing's bright intelligence chief, told his French counterparts that another German offensive was about to be launched. The French were unimpressed. What did a green American know about such

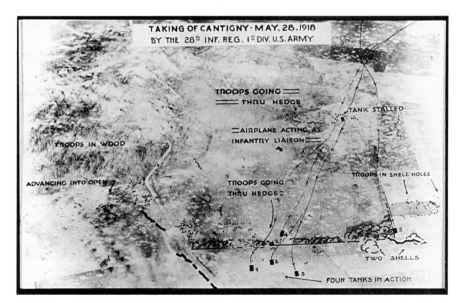

9-18 Overview of the taking of Cantigny, May 28, 1918, by the 28th Infantry Regiment, 1st Division, U.S. Army.

9-19 Left to right: Brigadier General F. C. Marshall, Mrs. Theodore Roosevelt, Jr., Lieutenant Colonel Boswell, and Lieutenant Colonel Theodore Roosevelt, Jr., at Romagne, France.

9-20 German prisoners captured in July 1918 by the U.S. 9th and 23rd Infantry Regiments, 2nd Division, at Chateau Thierry, France.

things? However, Nolan was right, and soon Ludendorff struck with what became the Second Marne offensive. Tons of gas and high explosive shells landed on three French and three British frontline divisions. Next, artillery and mortar fire blasted various Allied headquarters, road junctions, and artillery positions.

Then came the assault, with seventeen divisions in the first wave and thirteen more in reserve.

The Allied lines crumpled, and by May 30 Ludendorff had reached the Marne River. General Henri Petain [9-22], a man for whom Pershing had great respect, asked for American divisions to help stem the tide. Of particular

9-21 Barbed-wire receiving station crowded with German prisoners, Mesnit St. Firmin, France, May 1918.

9-22 Marshal Petain.

9-23 Men of the 26th Infantry, 1st Battalion, on their way to the front in Maron, France, April 6, 1918.

9-24 Men of the 2nd Marine Division, led by Major J. S. Turrill en route to a rest camp after sixteen days at the front, Chateau Thierry, France, June 18, 1918.

importance was the area near Chateau Thierry, only forty miles northeast of Paris, which represented the tip of a German salient threatening the French capital itself. American capabilities, however, were limited. Of those divisions not committed, only the 2nd and 3rd were within a reasonable distance of Chateau Thierry. Orders were issued, and both divisions were soon headed in that direction, moving either by rail or truck [9-23, 9-24], then advancing on foot through a series of forced marches [9-25],

passing through a muddy, torn-up, tangled countryside [9-26, 9-27]. Despite the difficulties, the troops managed to be in position to meet the next German thrust.

The 2nd Division, commanded by Major General Omar Bundy [9-28], was the only one of Pershing's original four that had been organized in France rather than the United States. After being formed in late October 1917 and undergoing training, it was first committed to a quiet sector in March 1918. Bundy's division was unique in

that it contained a brigade of Marines comprised of the 5th and 6th Marine Regiments. The brigade was now commanded by Pershing's former chief-of-staff, James Harbord, who had begged to serve in a line rather than a staff position. The opportunity came when the Marine brigade commander, Brigadier General Charles Doyen [9-29], was found physically unfit for combat duty. During the change in command ceremony, the Marines had assured Harbord that they would live up to their

9-25 Reserves of the 16th Infantry, 1st Division, going into action near Chaudon, France, July 16, 1918.

9-26 Bridge across the Aire River blown up by retreating Germans. Note the temporary footbridge built by engineers of the 1st Division. Floville, France, October 1918.

9-27 American troops in the ruins of the village of Lahayvillo, September 1918.

motto of "semper fidelis" (always faithful) and be happy to serve under an Army officer. They would not let Harbord down, nor he them. In the weeks ahead, Harbord showed great loyalty to his Marines, even tak-

9-29 Brigadier General Charles Doyen.

ing their part if a dispute arose with his fellow Army officers.

The 2nd Division was now headed for its first serious action, and it considered itself ready. That was especially true for the Marine brigade, which unlike other AEF regiments had a large percentage of regulars, many of whom had served with their unit for years. Soon the 2nd Division had arrived in the Chateau Thierry sector, near the village of Vaux and a small forest nearby, Belleau Wood. The corps commander controlling that sector was a veteran French colonial, General Jean DeGoutte. With the situation desperate, De-Goutte proposed sending American units into the battle one at a time, under French command, as he had done with the previous units. That would not do, argued the Americans. They were strung out along the road, tired and hungry, lacking artillery and machine guns, and carrying only one hundred rounds of ammuni-

tion per man. A better plan, they said, would be to establish an American defensive line behind the French and then hold that line as the French came back through. The weary DeGoutte somewhat reluctantly agreed to the American counterplan. Accordingly, Bundy's men took up a position in depth behind the French 43rd Division. On the right was the Division's 3rd Brigade, and on the left was the Marine Brigade. In addition, to shore up the left flank temporarily, Bundy assigned Colonel Paul "Follow Me" Malone's 23rd Infantry Regiment [9-30].

The serious fighting that took place during the days ahead was something that no one involved would ever forget. Although the Americans initially were not in direct contact with the enemy, they nevertheless spent a

9-30 Colonel Paul B. Malone.

9-31 Drawing by Captain W. Morgan depicting a dugout of the 5th Marines in Bois de Belleau (Belleau Wood).

miserable three days amid mud, rain, and constant shelling that caused considerable casualties. By June 4, 1918, the French had fallen back and turned the sector over to the Americans.

With Ludendorff's offensive having run out of steam, Foch launched a counterattack on June 6 with everything he had, including the American 2nd and 3rd Divisions. The Marine Brigade, part of the 2nd, attacked at Belleau Wood, with the first objective being Hill 142. Due to a lack of proper reconnaissance, it was assumed that Hill 142 was either unoccupied or lightly held, and once 142 was secured, Belleau Wood should be easily taken. This was not the case, and the attacking Marines, going forward in waves, were cut down ruthlessly by German machine guns. In effect, the initial assault, and the ensuing attack on Belleau Wood,

was badly bungled, causing huge numbers of needless casualties. Never had American troops of any age performed more courageously, however. War correspondent Floyd Gibbons wrote, "I never saw men charge to their death with finer spirit." Gunnery Sergeant Dan Daly, who already held two Medals of Honor—from the Boxer Rebellion of 1900 and the occupation of Haiti in 1915—was said to have urged his men forward by shouting, "Come on, you sons of bitches, do you want to live forever?"

To the right of the Marines, the division's 3rd Brigade met stiff resistance and suffered heavy losses. In all, the 2nd Division casualties numbered 9,777, including 1,811 dead, more casualties than any comparable American unit had suffered since the Civil War. But Belleau Wood was finally secured. Oddly

enough, through a censor's mistake, only Floyd Gibbons's story describing the Marine action got through. The army participation went unreported, and the Marines received full credit for Belleau Wood. Rather than being reported as a disaster, the headlines read, "U.S. MARINES SMASH HUN" and "GREAT CHARGE OVERTHROWS CRACK FOE FORCES." Nevertheless, Belleau Wood is a proud chapter in Marine Corps history, not because of the tactical results, but because of the Leathernecks' unparalleled valor [9-31, 9-32].

Ludendorff's next offensive was aimed at an area northwest of Chateau Thierry. Foch was defending that area by the weakened French Fifth Army, reinforced by the U.S. 3rd Division on the right of the line. The 3rd Division was commanded by Major General Joseph T. Dickman [9-33], an able, active leader, known as "a staunch friend of the enlisted man," with a bulky appearance that was misleading. This former cavalryman, who had spent his early career on the frontier fighting Indians, was well prepared for the task ahead. By May 30, 1918, he had deployed his division along the Marne River near Chateau Thierry. The critical point, on the right of the line, was the Surmelin Valley defended by Dickman's 30th and 38th Infantry Regiments.

The month of June and the first part of July were relatively quiet for the 3rd Division, giving it time to fortify and to establish a defense in depth, not only along the river but on two key ridgelines [9-34, 9-35]. By interrogating prisoners [9-36], it was learned that Ludendorff would launch his attack on the Marne early on July 15. Accordingly, on the night of the 14th, as two

9-32 Another drawing by Captain W. Morgan showing men of the 5th Division near Montreuil. The woods where the men were encamped were still in range of the German guns. The men built dugouts in which they would disappear at the first sound of trouble.

9-33 Major General J. T. Dickman (center) with aides leaving the headquarters of the 1st Division. Nonsard, France, September 1918.

9-34 Private Albert V. Lems, of the 32nd Division, on duty in an observation post at Lock 25 on the canal at Eglingen, Alsace, Germany, June 1918.

German divisions assembled for the attack, the Americans fired a massive artillery barrage, disrupting formations and inflicting heavy casualties. The Germans, following a barrage of their own, hit in force early on the 15th. Fighting was fierce, the line buckled, and eventually the Americans were driven back several thousand yards. Gamely they counterattacked, and by the end of the day the line had stiffened and straightened. Although

9-35 A trench built through rock by Company A, 2nd Engineer, between Menil la Tour and Andilly, France, March 1918.

9-36 Private Kraus (front), 272nd Infantry, German Army, captured by the 1st Division, being taken to an interrogation center, Mesnil St. Firmin, France, May 1918.

9-37 Men of the 18th Machine Gun Battalion, 1st Division, enjoying a game of cards during a few moments of rest, Petit Froissy, France, May 1918.

9-38 Men of the 18th Infantry Regiment, 1st Division, washing their feet after a hike, April 1918.

fighting continued throughout the 16th, by the end of the 15th Ludendorff knew his latest offensive had failed. It came at a severe price, but the 30th and 38th Infantry had justly earned for the division the proud title, "Rock of the Marne." Now the 3rd Division could mourn its dead, gather its strength for the next action, and take time to relax [9-37, 9-38].

TEN

The Air War

The Air War

In December 1903 the Wright brothers accomplished the world's first heavier-than-air flight [10-1]. Aviation made rapid strides in the next few years, but it took World War I for it to gain real prominence, with the demands of war turning the plane into a weapon of death. Ironically, as Britain, France, and Germany were developing a military air arm, the United States, home of the Wright brothers, was left far behind. For example, when Pershing was chasing Pancho Villa in Mexico, his six reconnaissance planes all crashed, wiping out the entire U.S. Air Service. In May 1917, shortly after America entered the war, the French had 1,700 planes at the front. By contrast, the United States then owned but fifty-five planes, of which fifty-one were obsolete and four were obsolescent. In Pershing's words, "The situation at that time as to aviation was such that every American ought to feel mortified to hear it mentioned. . . ."

10-1 The Wright brothers prepare for the world's first flight, December 17, 1903, at Kitty Hawk, North Carolina.

Early fighter planes were made of wood, canvas, and wire, heavily loaded with gasoline. Many of these flimsy planes crashed even before entering combat; there was, for example, a likelihood that too steep a dive might rip the wings to shreds. Moreover, most early flyers took to the air without benefit of a parachute. It took a brave man even to fly, and an even braver one to go aloft when the air war evolved into midair duels to the death, and pilots began measuring their life expectancy in weeks.

In the early days of the war, planes were used for reconnaissance, and it was not uncommon for Allied and German fliers to wave at each other as they went on their respective missions. Then, so the story goes, someone took a pistol aloft and took a pot-shot at an enemy plane. The first true air combat, however, took place on October 5, 1914, when two French aviators shot down a German plane. It soon became common for planes to carry machine guns mounted on swivels,

10-2 A machine gun used by Americans on French airplanes during World War I.

10-3 Hermann Goering with forward-mounted machine gun.

with rear-seat airmen firing at their opponents [10-2].

It was only after Anthony Fokker, a Dutch inventor who worked for the Germans, developed a sychronizing mechanism permitting guns to fire straight ahead without chewing up the propeller, that aerial combat came of age. A forward-mounted machine gun is shown is photo 10-3. Interestingly, the pilot in 10-3 is the future Reich-marshal Hermann Goering, whom Americans remember from World War II as the corpu-lent head of the Nazi Luftwaffe and an infamous member of Adolf Hitler's inner circle.

By the time America entered the war, aerial warfare had acquired a sort of romantic aura. Recruiting posters urged young men to sign up to "become an American eagle," and everyone knew of Manfred von Richthofen, the "Red Baron," who was begrudgingly admired, even by his enemies, and who shot down some eighty Allied planes or balloons before he himself was killed [10-4].

For America in 1917, aerial capability required a hasty attempt to catch up. Planes were acquired, often by purchase from the Allies, hangars were built [10-5], and airfields were constructed both at home and

10-4 The Red Baron, Manfred von Richthofen.

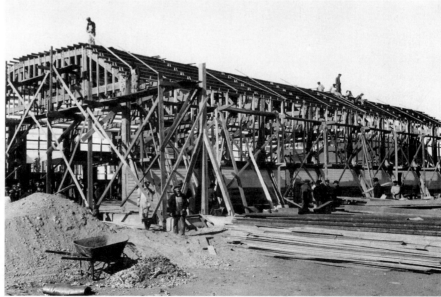

10-5 A typical hanger built by Americans to house a future American air fleet (the war was over before they were used).

10-6 An airfield where American pilots were trained.

10-7 Curtis JN4-D.

10-8 French Nieuport XI.

abroad [10-6]. Initially the Air Service was part of the Signal Corps, but in March 1918 it became a separate branch of the Army. Air cadets were trained in the Curtis JN4-D, known as the "Jenny" [10-7]. Later in France, they switched to the French Nieuport XI [10-8]. Volunteer instructors came from both France and England; one was Vernon Castle, the world-famous dancer, who with his wife Irene had popularized the Castle Walk, Turkey Trot, Fox Trot, and the One-Step. As a member of the Royal Flying Corps, Vernon Castle had shot down two enemy planes. In February 1918, he was killed at Taliaferro Field in Texas in a midair collision with a plane flown by a cadet.

In the combat zone, chief of the American Air Service was the flamboyant maverick William B. (Billy) Mitchell [10-9]. His boss,

10-9 General Billy Mitchell.

10-10 General Benjamin Foulois.

overall chief of the Air Service, was General Benjamin Foulois, an aviation pioneer who had flown reconnaissance for Pershing in Mexico [10-10].

When the United States declared war, the most experienced American pilots were not in their own country's service, but were serving in France as volunteer members of the Lafayette Escadrille, a unit formed in April 1916 with thirty-eight Americans, some transfers from the French Foreign Legion, and four French officers who trained them to fly pursuit planes. Their numbers would soon grow as other volunteers rushed to join what was perceived as a glorious adventure. With America still at peace, the French welcomed the young American volunteers with enthusiasm, providing them with the finest equipment and accommodations. At their station in Bar-le-Duc, the high-spirited Americans created almost a country club atmosphere, with parties, drinking, and poker games. Their carefree reputation was further enhanced when they acquired two lion cub mascots that they named "Whiskey" and "Soda."

The war, however, would soon become serious business for members of the Lafayette Escadrille—for some, deadly serious. Of the 224 Americans who served in the unit, 11 died of illnesses or in accidents, 15 became prisoners of war, and 51 died in combat. Eleven of them became "aces"—an "ace" being a flyer who shot down at least five enemy planes.

In December 1917, American pilots of the Lafayette Escadrille were transferred to the American Air Service. In February the Escadrille became the 103rd Aero Squadron. By the following April, the United States had three squadrons in active service, two for observation and one for pursuit. One of the latter was the 94th, known as the "Hat in the Ring" Squadron. Its insignia, an Uncle Sam Hat in a loop, symbolized America's entry into the war [10-11].

Several former members of the Lafayette Escadrille came to serve as flying instructors and advisers, one of whom was the colorful Raoul Lufberry [10-12]. Lufberry, son of a French mother and an American father, had begun his aviation career in 1911

10-11 Two airmen and a plane displaying the "Hat in the Ring" squadron symbol.

10-12 Raoul Lufberry (left) and another member of the Lafayette Escadrille.

when he became mechanic for French pilot Marc Pourpe. The pair barnstormed their way through China, Japan, India, and Egypt, finally landing in Paris just as war broke out. Pourpe joined the French Air Service, and Lufberry came along as his mechanic. To avenge Pourpe's death at the end of 1914, Lufberry applied for pilot training and earned his wings. He joined other American pilots in the Lafayette Escadrille and scored his first kill in August 1916. By the end of 1917, Lufberry was a leading ace, with seventeen official kills. In May 1918, while flying a Nieuport in pursuit of a German Albatross [10-13], he received a tracer bullet in his gas tank. His plane burst into flames, and Lufberry, preferring a quick ending rather than a flaming one, jumped to his death.

The first day of operations for the 94th Aero Squadron was Sunday, April 14, 1918. That day two German Pfalzes, the best German airplanes at the time, set out to teach the American newcomers a lesson [10-14]. Within four minutes, both Pfalzes had been shot down. The battle was seen by those on the ground, and Billy Mitchell said the double victory "had a more important effect on American fighting aviation than any other single occurrence. It gave our men a confidence that could have been obtained in no other way."

The most famous member of the 94th was undoubtedly the

10-13 A German Albatross.

10-14 Bi-winged German Pfalz scouts.

10-15 Captain Eddie Rickenbacker of the 94th Hat in the Ring squadron was credited with bringing down twenty-two enemy aircraft.

10-16 Rickenbacker (fourth from the right) and others receiving medals.

10-17 Quentin Roosevelt next to a German Fokker D VII aircraft.

ace. At the end of the war, by which time he commanded the 94th, Eddie Rickenbacker was the leading American ace, with sixty-nine victories, of which twenty-six were credited to him personally. He was applauded at home and abroad and received many awards, both from America and her Allies [10-16]. His decorations included the Medal of Honor (received in 1931), the Distinguished Service Cross with nine oak leaf clusters, the French Legion of Honor, and the Croix de Guerre with four palms.

On July 14, 1918, Quentin Roosevelt, youngest son of the former president, was shot down and killed by German ace Christian Denhauser [10-17]. He was rendered full military honors, his plane's wheels and propeller were set over the grave, and a graveside service was conducted by Father Francis P. Duffy, chaplain of the 165th Infantry Regiment, a unit better known as the "Fighting 69th" of the New York National Guard [10-18]. Eddie Rickenbacker described Quentin as "gay, hearty, and absolutely square in everything he said or did."

Pershing wrote a letter to the grief-stricken father saying, "Quentin died as he had lived, and served, nobly and unselfishly, in the full strength and vigor of his youth, fighting the enemy in clean combat. You may well be proud of your gift to the nation in his supreme sacrifice."

German propaganda made much of Quentin's death,

former racing car driver, Eddie Rickenbacker [10-15]. His first assignment in France had been to serve as Pershing's chauffeur. Rickenbacker wanted to learn to fly, however, and though it took some pleading with Pershing, his transfer to the pursuit flying school at Cazaubon was finally

approved. After completing the course, he joined the "Hat in the Ring" Squadron, and on April 29, 1918, flying with James Normal Hall (coauthor of *Mutiny on the Bounty*), Rickenbacker scored his first victory. On May 30 he shot down his fifth plane to become the second American

10-18 Famous army chaplain, Father Duffy, conducting a service over the grave of Quentin Roosevelt.

10-19 The Spad Frank Luke would fly on his last mission.

bragging, "The greatest of living Americans sends his sons to fight against us, yet even they go down before the might of the Fatherland." America countered with, "Quite true, but where are the sons of the Kaiser?"

One of the most daring pursuit pilots was handsome, blond, twenty-one-year-old Frank Luke, who became known as the "Balloon Buster." Luke flew a Spad, a single-seat, single-engine, relatively slow fighter plane known for its ruggedness and high performance [10-19]. (Its name was derived from the initials of the *Societe pour l'Aviation et ses Derives*.) Shooting down a bal-

loon required both skill and courage. One had to fly low, becoming a target for enemy machine guns, then fire a tight-pattern burst into the top of the balloon, where most of the inflammable hydrogen was concentrated. With victories over both enemy aircraft and balloons, for a time Luke became America's leading ace. On September 29, after he downed three balloons and two Fokker pursuit planes [10-20], Luke's plane disappeared. Civilian witnesses on the ground testified that after crash landing, Frank Luke held off German soldiers with his pistol until he died of wounds. He became the

first American airman to be awarded the Medal of Honor, and no less a person than Eddie Rickenbacker called him "the greatest fighting pilot in the war."

Observation balloons had been known as early as the American Civil War, but it was in World War I that they came into full prominence. A balloon would be inflated [10-21], one or two courageous observers would study maps and climb into the basket [10-22], and then they would go aloft to report on enemy activity or to direct artillery fire [10-23]. If they came under attack, frantic ground crews would try to pull

10-20 A Fokker biplane.

10-21 An observation balloon.

10-22 The crew of an observation balloon from the 2nd Balloon Company near Mentreuil, France, July 1918.

10-23 Observation balloon of the 2nd Balloon Company ascending near Picardy Farm, France, July 1918.

down the tethered balloon quickly. On occasion, if the balloon burst into flames, the observers might try parachuting to safety [10-24].

As the number of available planes increased, aerial-massed formations became commonplace. For America's St. Mihiel operation, nearly 1,500 aircraft were placed under U.S. command. The large number of planes reflected the significance of the St. Mihiel attack to Allied

morale. It was important to everyone that this first American offensive be a success, and it was. Overall, however, those in charge of the Allied war effort considered St. Mihiel to be mainly a sideshow.

Be that as it may, at St. Mihiel forty-nine squadrons, twenty-nine of them American, were controlled by Billy Mitchell. This Allied armada strafed enemy positions and bombed the German rear areas.

It was the finest example to date of airplanes used en masse. Pershing, who was highly pleased with the operation, recommended Mitchell's promotion to brigadier general. He also wrote a warm commendation:

Please accept my sincere congratulations on the successful and very important part taken by the Air Force under your command on the first offensive of the American Army. The organization and control of the tremendous concentration of air forces . . . is as fine a tribute to you personally as is the courage and nerve shown by your officers a signal proof of the high morale which permeates the service under your command. . . . I am proud of you all.

In the air by this time was a bewildering variety of aircraft. The French developed and manufactured sixty-four types of observation, pursuit, and bombing planes. The British developed sixty-seven types, including the

10-24 Observer bailing out of a balloon near Meurtha-et-Moselle, France, November 1918.

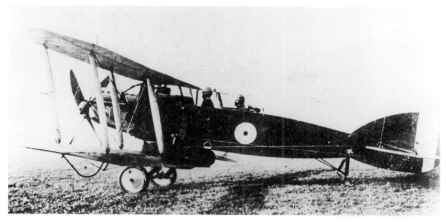

10-25 Bristol fighter.

10-26 A wrecked Sopwith Camel fighter.

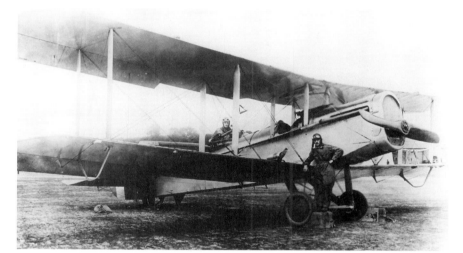

10-27 De Havilland DH4, the first American plane placed in France, June 1918.

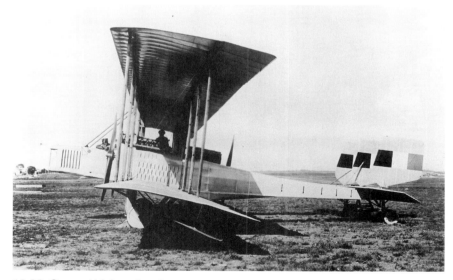

10-28 Caproni biplane bomber.

speedy Bristol Fighter [10-25] and the Sopwith Camel [10-26]. Comic strip readers may recall that the Sopwith Camel was "flown" by Snoopy from atop his doghouse as he imagined himself a heroic WW I flying ace. Meanwhile the only American-built plane to see action was the De Havilland DH4. The designers may have been proud of the DH4, but the pilots had other ideas, calling it the "flaming coffin" because of a gas tank located directly behind the pilot [10-27].

Some five hundred American cadets were trained at Foggia, Italy. Ninety-six of them would go on to serve at the front in Italian squadrons. In August 1918, Fiorello LaGuardia, an Italian-born congressman, later mayor of New York City, took charge of American pilots on the Italian front. Once in action, Major LaGuardia flew a Caproni biplane bomber [10-28].

On the whole, it must be said that German planes were better,

10-29 A German Rumpler pursuit plane.

10-30 A German Gotha bomber.

10-31 A Fokker triplane.

since Germany had concentrated on making small numbers of excellent planes while the Allies made larger numbers of good planes. The German Rumpler, for example, was an outstanding pursuit plane [10-29], and the Gotha Bomber [10-30] was highly effective. But the most famous plane of its time, and perhaps the most feared fighter, was the Fokker triplane as flown by Manfred von Richthofen, the "Red Baron" [10-31].

By the end of the war, the U.S. Army Air Service had truly come of age. American pilots had brought down 755 enemy airplanes while suffering a loss of 357. It had not been easy. Of the Yank pilots who fought in France, a third had been killed.

ELEVEN

Meuse-Argonne, the Final Push:

August–November 1918

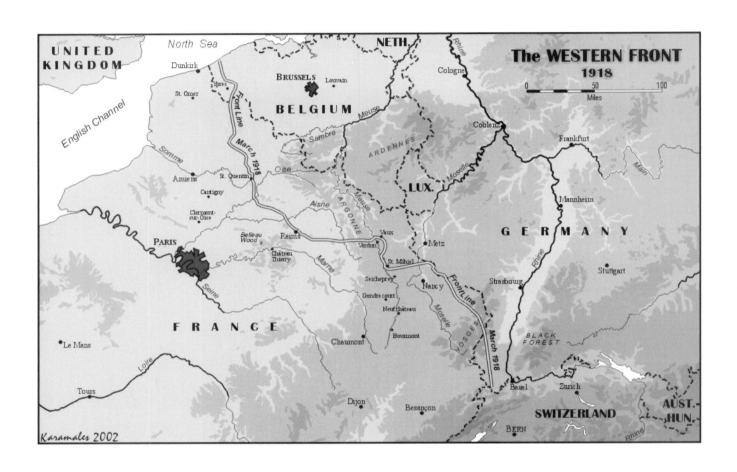

Meuse-Argonne, the Final Push:
August–November 1918

At Belleau Wood, Chateau Thierry, and St. Mihiel, the Americans, acting independently for the first time, had shown they could do the job. Not only were the Yanks pleased, the Allies, who had given the Americans full support, were similarly delighted. They knew the Doughboys were now capable of doing their full share.

For a time, it appeared the St. Mihiel attack might never take place. Foch had insisted that the attack be postponed so American divisions could be diverted to support his planned September offensive. Pershing had stood firm, insisting the St. Mihiel attack go as planned.

"There is one thing that must not be done," he said, "and that is to disperse the American forces among the Allied armies; the danger of destroying by such dispersion the fine morale of the American soldier is too great, to say nothing of the results to be obtained by using the American army as a whole."

Finally a compromise was reached. The St. Mihiel attack could go as planned, but two weeks later the Americans would also have to participate in the wider offensive in the Meuse-Argonne sector. Pershing agreed to the bargain, and two weeks later the Yanks were in place. It was a tricky maneuver, but a testimony to the growing professionalism of the AEF. This time, with so many divisions committed, it was necessary to decentralize control. Three new corps were established: Hunter Liggett's I Corps with the 4th, 26th, and 42nd Divisions [11-1]; and the trusty Robert Bullard's III Corps with the 3rd, 28th, and 32nd Division. Added later was V Corps, first under George Cameron, later Charles Sommerall.

Having blunted Ludendorff's thrust, Foch launched his grand counteroffensive in September 1918 with the rallying cry, "*Tout le monde à la bataille!*" To do

11-1 General Hunter Liggett (left) and General Robert Bullard (right).

11-2 A French 75mm Battery in action.

the job and break the Hindenburg line, he had at his disposal 220 divisions, with 160 on line and another 60 in reserve.

Pershing, now having more divisions under his command, established on October 11 the AEF First Army under Hunter Liggett and the Second Army under Robert Lee Bullard. For its part in the coming offensive, the American Army was

assigned a twenty-mile front in the difficult Meuse-Argonne sector, which contained three important military features: the heights above the east side of the Meuse River on the east; the Montfaucon Hills, 342 meters high, in the center; and the dense, heavily wooded Argonne Forest in the west.

In the Argonne, the Yanks had a huge advantage in manpower and artillery support. The

Germans, however, occupying ground they had been fortifying for months, had the advantage of terrain. They held a natural fortress, with impenetrable foliage and an underpinning of twisted, scratching brambles. One observer likened it to the Civil War battlefield called "The Wilderness." Another said this one was even worse. Although the German lines were mostly based on trenches, there were hundreds of machine-gun nests scattered throughout the sector, backed up by mortars and up to twenty feet of barbed wire.

At 2:30 A.M. on September 23, Allied guns began firing a rolling barrage, which to General Bullard sounded like the "collision of a million express trains." Overhead, circling in his Spad, Eddie Rickenbacker saw the twinkling lights of hundreds of guns and thought it resembled the opening of a major telephone switchboard [11-2]. Pershing envisioned a rolling barrage to support the attack, but everything soon broke down. A rolling barrage was only effective when troops could follow closely in its path. This time the troops were unable to keep up. Wherever Yanks went over the top [11-3, 11-4], they were met by a chatter of rifles and machine guns [11-5].

American casualties began piling up, and the lines became confused [11-6, 11-8]. Units found themselves out of contact, and the press dubbed one of

11-3 American troops going over the top.

11-4 American infantry advancing over open terrain, fall 1918.

11-5 German soldiers waiting in the trenches for Americans.

them "the Lost Battalion." In many cases the only communication was by means of homing pigeons. Of more than 15,000 pigeons trained to carry messages in France, some 5,000 disappeared—one suspects many of them went into French cooking pots. For the "Lost Battalion," however, one noble pigeon, "Cher Ami," won fame for getting through with the message that the battalion was being shelled by friendly fire [11-9].

By the end of the second day, the Germans had poured in reinforcements, the line had stiffened, and the attack had bogged down. Foch complained that the Americans were going too slow and even suggested shifting a French army into the American sector. Pershing would not hear of it [11-10]. He explained the difficult situation to Foch, only to be told, "I am interested only in results." After some argument, the Americans were allowed to resume the attack on their own terms [11-11, 11-12].

11-6 Wounded Doughboys being helped.

11-7 Stretcher bearers carrying wounded comrades of the 36th Division.

11-8 Stretcher bearers carrying a wounded man through the mud to safety.

11-9 "Cher Ami," the famous pigeon.

As the attacks continued, they were beginning to move more into open country, proving Pershing's wisdom in stressing fire and movement during the training. On October 8, 1918, the valorous Alvin C. York of Tennessee won the Congressional Medal of Honor and justly became famous both at home and abroad. York, a deeply religious man, had enlisted in the army only after his appeal for deferment as a conscientious objector was twice refused. His platoon, part of the 82nd Division's 328th Infantry Regiment, was

11-10 Foch (left) and Pershing.

On the night of September 25 a three-hour preliminary barrage began firing into back areas. Lieutenant Colonel George Patton [11-13], about to lead a tank attack, wrote his wife, "Just a word to you before I leave to play a part in what promises to be the biggest battle of the war or the world so far." After performing well, he was seriously wounded and evacuated only two days later.

11-11 Two Yanks setting out on a trench raid. Around their necks are canvas bags holding grenades.

11-12 Withdrawing from the front, men of the 16th Infantry Regiment, 1st Division, coming over a hill marching to Meuse, France, November 1918.

11-13 Lieutenant Colonel George Patton.

11-14 Sergeant Alvin C. York.

11-15 Tanks helped break through the Hindenburg line.

participating in the Meuse-Argonne offensive in northeastern France when it suffered heavy casualties at the hands of a nest of German machine gunners. York, leading seven men, fearlessly charged the nest of gunners, showering them with bullets. He killed 25, captured 132, and took 15 machine guns. Pershing would later call Alvin York "the greatest civilian soldier of the war [11-14]." "Here at last," Pershing said, "after 17 months of effort, an American army was fighting under its own flag."

The spirit of the American attack took the Germans by surprise. Rather than the plodding, steady advances they had seen in the past, this time they were faced by Americans who came wildly forward in sudden rushes, rarely stopping to regroup.

Flying overhead, American ace Eddie Rickenbacker reported with boyish enthusiasm as he looked down and saw Doughboys use what he called frontier tactics. "They scurried from cover to cover," Rickenbacker said, "always crouching low as they ran. Throwing themselves flat, they would get their rifles into action and spray the Boche with more bullets until they withdrew from sight. Then another running advance and another furious pumping of lead from the Yanks." Retreating Germans compared the Americans to "wild American Indians" and feared they might be scalped if captured.

The Hindenburg line was beginning to crack [11-15], and Erich Ludendorff recognized it as soon as anyone, perhaps sooner. He gave the order to start pulling back and asked his chief-of-staff to begin talking with the Allies about terms.

Suddenly it was over, an order to cease fire given at 11 A.M. on November 11, the

11-16 Yanks celebrate the armistice, November 11, 1918.

11-17 American sailor (second from left) and Red Cross nurse (second from right) with two French soldiers celebrating the armistice.

soon-to-be famous "11th hour of the 11th day of the 11th month" [11-16, 11-17]. In this final offensive, the total strength of the American First Army, including 135,000 French troops, reached 1,031,000 men. It suffered about 117,000 casualties but captured 26,000 prisoners, 874 guns, 3,000 machine guns, and large quantities of materiel. German casualties were estimated at 100,000. The Meuse-Argonne offensive, said Pershing, "stands out as one of the great achievements in the history of American arms."

Before long, American soldiers, artillery, and equipment were on their way home. Horses, which were an asset during the war, now became a burden as they were loaded onto trains [11-18] eventually to be transported home. Rifles were collected and put back into storage [11-19].

11-18 A horse being loaded onto train on the way to victory celebration in Paris.

11-19 U.S. 1st Division troops with arms stacked on street facing the Rhine River, Boppard, Germany, December 10, 1918.

All over Europe Americans were welcomed and cheered. In Luxembourg they were greeted with open arms [11-20 to 11-22], and in France the people were ecstatic to see them [11-23, 11-24]. The troops even had time to visit such shrines as the birthplace of Joan of Arc [11-25]. Surprisingly, even in defeated Germany, the troops received a warm welcome [11-26]. In the early days following the war, American soldiers were awarded many medals for valor and heroism throughout Europe [11-27 to 11-30].

Thousands of men lost their lives in Europe and many of their bodies remain there today [11-31, 11-32]. Their families chose not to send their bodies home; instead they remain with their fallen comrades in cemeteries throughout Western Europe. For those who did not return, John McRae said it well in his famous poem, "In Flanders Fields":

In Flanders Fields the poppies blow
Between the crosses, row on row
That mark our place, and in the sky

The larks, still bravely singing, fly
Scarce heard among the guns below.

We are the Dead. Short days ago
We lived, felt dawn, saw sunset glow,
Loved and were loved, and now we lie
In Flanders Fields.

Take up our quarrel with the foe
To you from falling hands we throw
The torch, be yours to hold it high
If ye break faith with us who die
We shall not sleep, though poppies grow
In Flanders Fields.

11-20 Citizens standing in front of a store in Luxembourg welcoming the arrival of the U.S. 18th Infantry Regiment, 1st Division, as they march along the main street, November 20, 1918.

11-21 General Pershing (left) and the Grand Duchess of Luxembourg (second from left) along with several other generals reviewing the 18th Infantry, 1st Division, as they pass the Grand Palace, November 20, 1918.

11-22 Crowds on the main street of Luxembourg welcoming men of the 18th Infantry, 1st Division, as they march through the city, November 20, 1918.

11-23 French troops parade through Paris, France, July 4, 1919.

11-24 Children watching and welcoming the 28th Regiment of the 1st Infantry Division liberating Cheveauges, France, from the Germans, November 8, 1918.

11-25 Members of the 28th Infantry, 1st Division, at the statue of Joan of Arc, Treveray, France.

11-26 U.S. 18th Infantry, 1st Division, crossing the Mosselle River into Muhl, Germany, December 1, 1918.

11-27 General Pershing (front and center) and General Charles Sommerall (left) with officers of the 1st Division reviewing men who were decorated with the Distinguished Service Cross, Vertuzey, France, November 20, 1918.

11-28 Left to right: Major General Edward T. McGlachlin, Marshall Petain, Major General Allen, and Major General Robert L. Howze, Coblenz, Germany, July 18, 1919.

11-29 Lieutenant Colonel G. E. Freeman decorating two sergeants for bravery, Neymont, France. November 17, 1918.

11-30 Left to right: Captain Sidney Graves, Corporal Robert Winkler, and Private J. A. Jarvis, who received the Croix de Guerre for bravery.

11-31 Tyne Cot Cemetery, Ypres, Belgium.

11-32 Aisne-Marne American Cemetery near Belleau, France.

TWELVE

The Aftermath

The Aftermath

Thus, the war to end all wars ended with death, debt, and destruction. And now the winning powers were ready to meet at Versailles to discuss what to do in the postwar period. It was a different world now: gone were the emperors and the rulers that governed Europe and much of the world from the fifteenth century to 1918. The Hohenzollern family of Prussia and Wilhelm II of Germany, the Hapsburgs and Franz Joseph of Austria, the Romanovs and Nicholas II of Russia, and the Ottomans of Turkey. These monarchies had kept some semblance of peace in Europe between 1815 and 1914 through the creation of the Concert of Europe, an informal balance of power among Europe's great powers. In their place was a new group of leaders, each with a different and personal agenda.

The "Big Four" [12-1], as they were dubbed, sought to change the face of Europe. France's Georges Clemenceau, "The Tiger" [12-2], was bent on revenge. He wanted to punish

12-1 "The Big Four": David Lloyd George of Britain, Vittorio Orlando of Italy, Georges Clemenceau of France, and Woodrow Wilson of the United States.

Germany for all its actions over the past half century against the French and to make sure that Germany would never rise again. He wished to deprive Germany of her colonies and her industrial might and to demilitarize her and surround her with buffer states. Prime Minister David Lloyd George [12-3] wanted to maintain the British Empire and British hegemony on the continent and around the world. Vittorio Orlando of Italy [12-4] sought to gain for Italy territory

12-2 Georges Clemenceau.

12-3 David Lloyd George.

12-4 Vittorio Orlando.

12-5 Woodrow Wilson.

and possessions that he believed were rightly hers, including colonies in Africa and the cities of Trieste and Fiume, which were given to Yugoslavia instead and would have provided Italy with ports on the coast of the Adriatic Sea. Lastly, Woodrow Wilson [12-5] wanted to play the honest broker; he wanted to re-organize Europe and the world with his famous Fourteen Points. These points in brief sought openly arrived at treaties, free trade, freedom of the seas, a restoration of Poland with its own access to the seas, a redrawing of the eastern boundaries of Europe based on self-determination, and the elimination of all German colonies also based on self-determination. The cornerstone of his Fourteen Points was the creation of the League of Nations, an organization that he believed would help govern and solve the world's problems and guarantee that a war like World War I would never happen again.

While the peace conference was going on and the arguments and disagreements between the Big Four were taking place, U.S. military men and women were coming home. All over the

12-6 The 16th Infantry Regiment led by Lieutenant Colonel C. R. Huebner passing through the victory arch in New York City's Washington Square Park, September 15, 1919.

12-7 The New York City victory parade as seen from Fifth Avenue and East 82nd Street, September 15, 1919. Viewing the parade from this vantage point were Secretary of War Newton Baker, Mayor of New York J. F. Hylan, and ex-Secretary of the Treasury William G. McAdoo.

United States, in every town, hamlet, and city, they were honored with celebrations and large parades. The first big celebration took place in New York City with soldiers marching, bands playing, crowds cheering, and politicians praising [12-6 to 12-8]. The celebration soon spread to Washington, D.C., where the crowds were just as vocal and adamant [12-9 to 12-12]. Ironically, though the war was over, vehicles and trains carrying returning soldiers from New York to Washington were marred by many accidents, as if they were still in combat somewhere in Europe [12-13, 12-14].

12-8 Left to right: unidentified, General Barry Rodman Wanamaker, unidentified, Chief-of-Staff General Marsh, Governor Smith, Mayor Hylan, unidentified, and others in the reviewing stand, September 15, 1919.

12-9 General John Pershing in a victory parade passing the Peace Monument in Washington, D.C., September 17, 1919.

The Paris peace conference was also marred by much bickering among the great powers who, while paying homage to Wilson, made fun of him behind his back and fought him over every line and paragraph of his Fourteen Points. The peace conference had some very notable men who later played key roles in world history, among them John Maynard Keynes [12-15], who would write about the economic consequences of the peace, and John Foster Dulles, who became secretary of state for the United States in later years.

12-10 The 18th Infantry Regiment marching in the Washington, D.C., victory parade.

12-11 The entire 18th Infantry Regiment grouped on the U.S. Capitol steps, September 17, 1919.

12-12 View of 18th Infantry Regiment tractors coming up Pennsylvania Avenue, September 17, 1919.

12-13 A Cole Eight luxury car "side swiped" by a truck of the 1st Division supply train while en route from New York City to Washington, D.C., to participate in the parade, September 15, 1919.

fight led by Senator Henry Cabot Lodge of Massachusetts [12-16] and the journalist William Randolph Hearst [12-17], Wilson was defeated overwhelmingly by a senate vote. Soon after his defeat, the Hearst paper chain, on November 20, 1919, voiced the opinion of the opposition in newspaper editorials all over the country:

Wilson was willing to give in on certain parts of his Fourteen Points, but the one that he would not budge on was the League of Nations. He was able to sell the League to his European colleagues and adversaries, but in the United States it was another matter. Here he met opposition from senators who did not want to give up the sovereignty of the United States to foreign powers and who believed that the United States should do as the father of their country, George Washington, advised: "stay out of European alliances and entanglements." In a bitter

Thanks be to God, this nation had indeed had a new birth of freedom! The treaty is dead! . . . Congratulations to the Senators who have so manfully and victoriously fought the long and hard fight for America . . .

These are great days for the republic—glorious, gallant, splendid, wonderful days! They will live forever in the annals of the American people. We speak with a full heart and to celebrate only the victory of Americanism . . .

Once again our own flag floats

12-14 Wreck of a liberty truck of the 1st Division while en route from New York City to Washington, D.C. This truck ran off the road on a steep grade and a bad turn. September 15, 1919.

12-15 John Maynard Keynes.

12-16 Sen. Henry Cabot Lodge.

12-17 William Randolph Hearst.

12-18 Warren G. Harding.

alone, and undiminished by the company of other banners above our American land.

We need not be ashamed to read the proclamation of our famous Declaration, the mandates and inhibitions of our Constitution . . . and splendid ideals of that bright succession

12-19 Adolf Hitler.

of American presidents which begins with the name of Washington and ends with the name of Roosevelt.

Thus the treaty was dead in the United States, and the greatest nation on earth, which went into the war as a debtor nation and came out with more income than the next nineteen nations combined, went into isolation. However, Wilson did not give up, and for months he campaigned vigorously for the League. But on September 26, 1919, in Pueblo, Colorado, he fell victim to a stroke and never fully recovered. He died in February 1924. Congress never signed the Versailles Treaty and never voted to join the League of Nations. On May 20, 1920, the U. S. Congress, by joint resolution, declared the war over. James Cox, the Democratic nominee, ran on a platform to

join the League of Nations, but was defeated soundly by Warren G. Harding [12-18]. Harding put an end to Wilson's crusade by sounding its death warrant on February 7, 1923, with a famous speech that ended with the words "the League is not for us." For the next nineteen years a new world order—one that was not so nice and full of chaos—was created. Dictators emerged all over Europe, among them two that would reshape the world and help plunge it into another great war some twenty years later, Adolf Hitler [12-19] and Joseph Stalin [12-20].

Hence the war to end all wars ended up in actuality being a twenty-year truce that led to World War II, the greatest war in history. In the words of one songwriter many years later about a different war, "Where have all the

12-20 Vladimir Lenin (left) and Joseph Stalin (right).

soldiers gone? Long time passing. Where have all the soldiers gone? Long time ago. Where have all the soldiers gone? Gone to graveyards every one. . . . When will we ever learn? When will we ever learn?"

Chronology

1914

June 28	Archduke Franz Ferdinand and his wife are assassinated
July 23	Austria-Hungary sends ultimatum to Serbia
July 28	Austria-Hungary declares war on Serbia
August 1	Russia's armed forces begin to mobilize for war
August 1	Germany declares war on Russia
August 3	Germany declares war on France
August 4	U.K. declares war on Germany and its allies
August 26–30	Battle of Tannenberg
September 5–10	German offensive halted at First Battle of the Marne
October 12–November 11	First Battle of Ypres

1915

April 25	Allied forces land at Gallipoli
May 7	German U-Boat sinks the *Lusitania*
December	Evacuation of Gallipoli begins

1916

February 21–December 18	Battle of Verdun
May 31–June 1	Battle of Jutland
July 1–November 19	Battle of the Somme
November 7	Woodrow Wilson reelected president of the U.S.

1917

February 1	Germans reopen unrestricted submarine warfare
March 1	Zimmerman Telegram made public
March 15	Russia's Czar Nicholas II abdicates
April 3	President Wilson asks Congress to declare war against Germany
April 6	U.S. formally declares war on Germany
May 19	President Wilson signs the Conscription Act into law
October 21	Three battalions of U.S. troops, placed under French command, become the first to enter service on the Western Front
October 24–November 10	Battle of Caporetto

| November 7 | Bolsheviks seize power in Russia |
| December 3 | Bolshevik government signs an armistice with Germany |

1918

March 3	Russia signs a separate peace, the Treaty of Brest-Litovsk
March 21	Germany launches its spring offensive on the Western Front
July 18	Final German offensive fails, Allied counteroffensive begins
November 9	Germany's Kaiser Wilhelm II abdicates
November 11	Germany signs an armistice with the Allies

1919

| January 18 | Versailles peace conference begins |
| June 28 | Treaty of Versailles signed |

Selected Bibliography

Albrecht-Carrié, René. *The Meaning of the First World War*. Engelwood Cliffs, N.J.: Prentice-Hall, 1965.

Berghahn, V. R. *Germany and the Approach of War in 1914*. New York: St. Martin's Press, 1973.

Czernin, Ferdinand. *Versailles, 1919: The Forces, Events and Personalities That Shaped the Treaty*. New York: G. P. Putnam's Sons, 1965.

Don Passos, John. *Nineteen Nineteen*. New York: Washington Square Press, 1930, 1961.

Eisenhower, John S. D. *Yanks: The Epic Story of the American Army in World War I*. New York: The Free Press, 2001.

Farwell, Byron. *Over There: The United States in the Great War 1917–1918*. New York: W. W. Norton & Co., 1999.

Ferro, Marc. *Nicholas II: Last of the Tsars*. Translated by Brian Pearce. New York: Oxford University Press, 1991.

Gilbert, Martin. *The First World War: A Complete History*. New York: Henry Holt and Co., 1994.

Hart, Captain B. H. Liddell. *The Real War: 1914–1918*. Boston: Little, Brown and Co., 1930.

Hillgruber, Andreas. *Germany and the Two World Wars*. Translated by William C. Kirby. Cambridge, Mass.: Harvard University Press, 1981.

Horn, Alistair. *The Price of Glory: Verdun 1916*. London: Penguin Books, 1962, 1993.

Hughes, Michael. *Nationalism and Society: Germany 1800–1945*. London: Edward Arnold, 1988.

Keegan, John. *The First World War*. New York: Alfred A. Knopf, 1999.

Koch, H. W., ed. *The Origins of the First World War: Great Power Rivalry and German War Aims*. London: Macmillan, 1990.

Kohn, George C. *Dictionary of Wars*. New York: Anchor Doubleday, 1986.

Lafore, Laurence. *The Long Fuse: An Interpretation of the Origins of World War I*. Philadelphia: J. B. Lippincott, 1971.

Laqueur, Walter, and George L. Mosse, eds. "1914: The Coming of the First World War." *Journal of Contemporary History*, vol. 3. New York: Harper and Row, 1966.

Lincoln, W. Bruce. *In War's Dark Shadow: The Russians Before the Great War*. New York: Oxford University Press, 1994.

Lincoln, W. Bruce. *Passage Through Armageddon: The Russians in War and Revolution, 1914–1918*. New York: Oxford University Press, 1994.

Lyons, Michael J. *World War I: A Short History*. Engelwood Cliffs, N.J.: Prentice-Hall, 1994.

Marks, Sally. *The Illusion of Peace: International Relations in Europe, 1918–1933*. New York: St. Martin's Press, 1976.

Marshall, S. L. A. *World War I*. American Heritage Library. Boston: Houghton Mifflin Co., 1964, 1992.

Massie, Robert K. *Dreadnought: Britain, Germany, and the Coming of the Great War*. New York: Random House, 1991.

Mead, Gary. *The Doughboys: America and the First World War*. New York: Overlook Press, 2000.

Paschall, Rod. *The Defeat of Imperial Germany, 1917–1918*. New York: Da Capo Press, 1994.

Remak, Joachim. *The Origins of World War I: 1871–1914*. New York: Holt, Rinehart and Winston, 1967.

Taylor, A. J. P. *A History of the First World War*. New York: Berkeley Publishing Corp., 1966.

Taylor, Edmond. *The Fall of the Dynasties: The Collapse of the Old Order, 1995–1922*. Garden City, N.Y.: Doubleday and Co., 1963.

Thomson, George Malcolm. *The Twelve Days: 24 July to 4 August 1914*. New York: G. P. Putnam's Sons, 1964.

Index

About the Authors

Donald M. Goldstein, Ph.D., is a retired U.S. Air Force lieutenant colonel, a professor of public and international affairs at the University of Pittsburgh, and a best-selling author. He is the coauthor of all the books in Brassey's America at War series.

The late **Harry J. Maihafer** was a retired U.S. Army colonel who commanded troops in the Korean War. He authored several books, including *War of Words: Abraham Lincoln and the Civil War Press* and *Brave Decisions: Profiles in Courage and Character from American Military History*.